Partial Memoirs

Catharine Savage Brosman, The Pelican Club,
Exchange Place, New Orleans, 2004

Partial Memoirs

Catharine Savage Brosman

GA

GREEN ALTAR BOOKS
SHOTWELL PUBLISHING

Published by GREEN ALTAR BOOKS, an imprint of
SHOTWELL PUBLISHING LLC
Post Office Box 2592
Columbia, So. Carolina 29202
www.ShotwellPublishing.com

Cover Image: "Chair." Oil on canvas. By Tommy Van Auken.

ISBN: 978-1-963506-26-6

FIRST EDITION

10 9 8 7 6 5 4 3 2 1

Produced in the Republic of South Carolina

Creative Work by Catharine Savage Brosman

Watering (Athens: University of Georgia Press, 1972);
Abiding Winter (Florence, KY: R. L. Barth, 1983) (chapbook);
Journeying From Canyon de Chelly (Baton Rouge: LSU Press, 1990);
The Shimmering Maya and Other Essays (Baton Rouge: LSU Press, 1994);
Passages (Baton Rouge: LSU Press, 1996);
The Swimmer and Other Poems
(Edgewood, KY: R.L. Barth, 2000) (chapbook);
Places in Mind (Baton Rouge: LSU Press, 2000);
Petroglyphs: Poems and Prose (Thibodaux, LA: Jubilee:
A Festival of the Arts, Nicholls State University, 2003) (chapbook);
The Muscled Truce (Baton Rouge: LSU Press, 2003);
Finding Higher Ground: A Life of Travels (Reno: University Press of Nevada, 2003);
Range of Light (Baton Rouge: LSU Press, 2007) ;
Breakwater (Macon: Mercer University Press, 2009);
Trees in a Park (Thibodaux, LA: Chicory Bloom Press, 2010) (chapbook);
Under the Pergola (Baton Rouge: LSU Press, 2011).;
On the North Slope (Macon: Mercer University Press, 2012);
On the Old Plaza (Macon: Mercer University Press, 2014);
Music from the Lake (Rockford, IL: Chronicles Press, 2017);
A Memory of Manaus (Macon: Mercer University Press, 2017);
An Aesthetic Education and Other Stories
(Columbia: Green Altar / Shotwell Publishing, 2019, 2022);
Chained Tree, Chained Owls: Quintains
(Columbia, SC: Green Altar / Shotwell Publishing, 2020);
Clara's Bees (UK: Little Gidding Press, 2021);
Arm in Arm (Macon: Mercer University Press, 2022);
Aerosols and Other Poems
(Columbia, SC: Green Altar / Shotwell Publishing, 2023.)

Forthcoming collections
Metates and Other Poems (Lafayette: University of Louisiana–Lafayette Press);
Fire in the Mind: Poems New and Selected (Macon: Mercer University Press).

For biographical summaries, see
Wikipedia in English and Wikipedia in French.

Acknowledgments

This book complements and parallels memoirs in the form of essays that I collected or published separately in the past, to which I refer readers. I am grateful to the press directors and periodical editors who brought out the following: *The Shimmering Maya and Other Essays* (Louisiana State University Press, 1994); *Finding Higher Ground: A Life of Travels* (University Press of Nevada, 2003); *Breakwater* (Mercer University Press, 2009); *Music from the Lake* (Chronicles Press, 2017); and "Aunt Flora in My Retroscope" (Phi Kappa Phi Forum, 2022). The opening paragraphs of chapter twelve are borrowed from the essay "Islands of Our Years," which appeared originally in the *Sewanee Review* and is collected in *Music from the Lake*. The passage is used by permission.

I should like to recognize my daughter, Kate Deimling, for help with various matters and selecting for chapter nine the photograph of her father as a young man; Eleanor P. Beebe and Olivia McNeely Pass, for reading the manuscript; James Miller, for giving me Phoebe Elliott Hill's travel diary and a photocopied family history centered on her, drawn up by his mother, the late Jean Hill Miller; Charlie Hill, for assisting me in tracing my grandparents' travels; and Nancy Van Auken and Sylvia Yarborough, for assistance with photographs.

The cover art, "Chair," oil on canvas (1994), by Tommy Van Auken, an award-winning painter in the Richmond, Virginia area, is reproduced by permission. His work can be seen online and on his Instagram page under the name tommyvanawkward.

Photograph credits are the following: Frontispiece, Joseph Warner; head shot in chapter ten, Thomas Vincent Van Auken, Jr. (the painter's father); photo in chapter eleven of the author reading, Melissa Bonin; portrait in chapter twelve of the author and Patric Savage, Olivia McNeely Pass. All are used by permission.

Contents

In memory of honored faces
and voices in my past who now are gone;
in gratitude for those in my present.

Chapter One

Introduction

A preface is an introduction to the *book*; an introduction presents the *subject*. In the present instance, book and subject are nearly the same, as is the case generally for what is called an intimate or personal memoir. Hence, the present title, despite material just below that is of more literary than personal application. To undertake a personal memoir is ipso facto to assert that the author's reminiscences, thus the author, constitute and warrant the enterprise. "I am myself the subject of my book," wrote Montaigne of his *Essais*. (True, true; but he went on a great length also about others and others' writing.)[1]

I shall try to unpack (as the cultural critics say) the title of this account.

The word *memoir* or *memoirs* can mean simply *history*, whether a broad or a limited one, presented from a personal point of view. The term has been used for Julius Caesar's *Gallic Wars*, various medieval French quasi-histories by military men, and the record offered by Marguerite de Valois, the first woman memoirist in France. While giving detailed historical information, often military, the memoir may exclude most private concerns except those that

---

[1]   In the eighteenth century, two centuries after Montaigne, the comte de Buffon identified similarly author and writing. "Le style est l'homme même" (the very man). Style (good or bad) makes the private man public.

1

impinge upon events. Think of the great twentieth-century figures de Gaulle, Eisenhower, and Churchill, who wrote the memoirs of their time and their roles in it. I give a stricter meaning to the word, without considering the question of singular versus plural except to say that breadth of undertaking appears to be the main distinction. The present narrative is concerned not with a swath of history but with me and my background—a narrow focus, though embracing a lifetime. It is thus closer to autobiography.

The two genres have loose parameters; they are like adjoining waters, blending into each other. Each may be in the form of a single, cohesive narrative, usually chronological, often with flashbacks and flash-forwards. Or it may consist of essays, sketches, or "moments" that, together, present various experiences of the author, cumulatively creating a period or a life. St. Augustine's *Confessions* are the prototype of Occidental and Christian autobiography. In French literature, the genre is as old as Rousseau, who adopted St. Augustine's title for his own narrative, and Stendhal, in *L'Autobiographie de Henri Brulard* and *Souvenirs d'égotisme*. In America, one must not forget Benjamin Franklin's *Autobiography*, which he called "Memoirs," nor that of Mark Twain, more a series of anecdotes than a conventional narrative. The following pages contain ruminations and extensive portraits as well as accounts.

For decades now, the personal memoir has been popular here and abroad and, with the *me* generation, has become even more so. It can be considered a major genre—certainly a money-maker for publishers. *The New York Times* site offers a list of the fifty best examples of the past fifty years. Whatever the formal characteristics, the type offers an outlet to political figures and others, such as high-profile basketball stars, who no longer occupy their former positions but retain fame and can publicize themselves retrospectively in a favorable light. For women in particular it has been serviceable. In the past it was sometimes based on oral accounts or original records written up by others. Today it is available to nearly all, perhaps with ghost-writing support. The enterprise is necessarily self-serving, even when what it recounts is not *prima facie* to the author's honor.

Rousseau made, of his confessions, his penitence and atonement. If the writing is justified at all, it is by itself.

To inquire what hubris leads me, as countless others have been led, to rely on that justification is legitimate. For me, the immediate pretext was offered when a close friend, who knows my writing well, encouraged me to launch the project. "We want more than what you furnished in your autobiographical essays," she said, in essence. Whether it is truly wanting remains to be seen.

As for the adjective *partial*, it emphasizes the selectivity and incompleteness of our recall. Recollections and any accounts thereof must always be subject to amplification, correction, and new errors. A memoir is not an extended reality show. Contemporaneous accounts, recorded evidence, and so on, while perhaps attesting roughly to what was said or done, still depend in the end on human testimony and thus are subject to error, at some juncture, by omission or commission. They are usually partial in the other sense, also: biased, self-serving. What the spotlight illuminates counts; the rest, equally pertinent perhaps, is in shadows.

The present narrative is intended as a lasting way of seeing, but without claim to exclusivity. It shines light on the woman who is composing it now and on the experiences that shaped her character and ideas. It incorporates such recollections as I have, but selectively and intended, I stress, as a partial record only. Information on matters I did not witness comes from written and oral sources. Readers will encounter genealogical information and sidebar-type snapshots of figures from the past. They have value as Americana as well as personal interest to me, but if they bore you from the outset, skip them.

You may recognize that certain areas into which memory might shine its torch have received treatment elsewhere in my prose or poetry, perceptively (I hope) and adequately for their context. Some facts and scenes must return here, for clarification, expansion, or reassessment, or simply to present a coherent picture. The risk to be run is *redites*, or repetition—doubtless with differences, even contradictions in the telling. When we change, things change.

More than fifty years ago, in his study *Le Pacte autobiographique*, Philippe Lejeune argued that autobiography is based on an agreement signed by the author: he will offer a detailed account of his life (or a significant portion of it, usually his youth) as a genuine record; he will include nothing invented. The basis is always to be truth, the details verifiable, if possible, or as close to human truth as memory and language allow. Readers are to take the biographer at his word. In this respect the genre is a variety of today's creative nonfiction—journalism that requires (some say) accuracy but allows for compression, rearrangement, interpretation, and even insertion of the author. Fictionalizing and mythologizing are generally excluded, although Stendhal indulged in it in his quasi-autobiographical works, as did Malraux in his *Antimémoires*.

There are, of course, other genres available to those who wish to make known aspects of their past. Some are naive, in the sense that the writers did not mean the text to be source material on their lives. Consider letters in the past, often published now as testimonies to an epoch but intended at the time only as private correspondence. Consider other written or oral attestations, including the inferior, mostly ephemeral present-day substitutes, emails, texts, telephone calls, and recordings, all of which are witnesses to the moment or look backward via summary of the past. Diaries, journals, agendas, and notebooks can serve the same purpose. These testimonies may have value in a court of law.

Fiction and drama are often autobiographical, perhaps highly so, but their express purpose is not to serve as a record. My own fiction, collected in *An Aesthetic Education and Other Stories* (2019, 2022), sheds considerable light on my personality and experience. The narratrix, Harriett D'Aquin, has family connections in Colorado, spent her formative years in West Texas, and studied art, with a specialization in French painting. She works at a museum (a stand-in for a university) in New Orleans and travels to France. Most of her responses to people, places, situations, and paintings reflect what my own would be. But, like the self glimpsed in poems, she cannot be considered a portrait, nor is the text a record. The other characters are either fabricated from whole cloth (Jacques, the French painter) or are modeled, like important characters in Proust's masterpiece, on various real men and women, their features recombined to create persuasive figures but not authentic portraits.

Films and still shots (such as those reproduced here) record only the moment; you cannot take a picture in the past, but may, of course, show re-enacted portions via costumes, settings, speech. They are suspect but may incorporate reliable elements. Voice-overs or printed titles may add to their quasi-realism.

Autobiographical poems were once and remain sometimes a perfectly respectable genre, from the Romantics to mid-twentieth-century American confessional poets and present writers. John Betjeman's *Summoned by Bells* (1960), a book-length poem in excellent blank verse, which covers the poet's youth through Oxford, illustrates masterfully what can be done. (One discovers that a schoolmaster of his was T.S. Eliot.) Even if not labeled as such, the mode is dominant now for legions of practitioners in schools and elsewhere who simply pour out lines, usually unstructured, on their lives, their miseries.

But no poem, even patently autobiographical in some respects, should be taken as a source in whole, only in details, at the most; poems are too synthetic to have exact testimonial validity. They tend to arise from a sensibility, not from facts. They are not records but constructs in which autobiographic materials may be shaped. While I have included here numerous references to poems of mine that reflect me, family members, and events in my life, still, reader, beware.

A last genre to be recalled is the personal or familiar essay (mentioned above in connection with its great, original practitioner, Montaigne), perhaps explicitly autobiographical or simply furnishing elements of a character and a life. Certain passages may be straight narrative, while others explore views or assess experiences; flights of fancy are tolerated. In my three collections of familiar essays, readers may find scenes and characters from my life and the lives of family members who appear below; there are, in addition, poetic and philosophical developments that would fit less well into the current narrative. In other words, the essay assumes no *pacte autobiographique* (even if understanding is established) between the author and the reader.

As a literary historian and biographer, I am familiar with these traditional models but am in no way bound by them. The following pages contain numerous portraits, including my own; some are extended, warranting whole chapters. As a Mannerist painter exaggerating his subjects' features, or any painter who sees the need to spotlight or reinforce features—a strong chin, piercing eyes, a commanding pose, an empty sleeve—I have highlighted certain features in order to give them their full due. Readers, like viewers, will understand.

There is little overt drama here, however. Think of all the roles I have *not* played, the sort that would attract attention and might appear in headlines: actress, politician, philanthropist, high-placed hostess, innovative scientist, explorer (of course not!). In my girlhood, people, at least those of certain classes and ethnic background, did not indulge in drama; what little came out was understated. ("Father," said my uncle Kenneth to my grandfather, a physician, when it was clear that his wife would die of her cancer, "Ethel is not going to get well.") The long-established prejudice in Europe and America, now turned on its head, against stage careers, particularly for women, still held in wide swaths of society.

Yet readers will find certain reflections of strife. Logical, Cartesian, I nevertheless understand the appeal of disorder. Or at least I have not kept it always at bay. The Greeks honored it in their contrasting of Apollo with Dionysius. Both are a source of art. Poetry, said Voltaire, is "un beau désordre." In classical drama and many later models, the predicated disorder in the family or kingdom ("Something is rotten in the state of Denmark") must be set right somehow. "There is a divinity which shapes our ends, / rough-hew them as we may." Consider various masterpieces of Greek and Italian sculpture. Consider much Romantic poetry, where the disorder is in hearts. In argumentation, order is imposed on disparate elements: statement, opposition, interrogation, concession, modification, qualified restatement, and additional rhetorical movements, featuring contraries and leading to new positions. The same holds for poetic rhetoric.

Bohemian habits and attitudes associated with art, which favor disorder or at least go against reigning order, are themselves oppositional statements. Extremists might suggest that *only* in disorder, or *la vie de Bohème*, can art flourish. That is historically false; anarchy does not favor productivity, and great poetry, painting, sculpture, and music have flowered under authoritarian rule and rigid social arrangements. One need not transgress, though many artists have done so. In twentieth- and twenty-first century American poetry, there is a trend toward the outrageous, fostered notably by Allen Ginsburg and the Beat poets. At a much higher level of achievement, however, stand poets with stable lives and bourgeois habits: Robert Frost, Wallace Stevens, and William Carlos Williams. I can mention also Stéphane Mallarmé, Paul Valéry, and St.-John Perse (the diplomat Alexis St-Leger Leger) in France. I feel no need to violate boundaries or even to dress like a bohemian. Attired in black, maybe, with long earrings, an extra ring or so, or a scarf with a Cézanne print, I have gone as far as need be.

Nineteenth-century biographies, autobiographies, and memoirs—and many later examples—tended to follow the principles set down by Hippolyte Taine in 1866, during the period of French realism and Naturalism, for historiography in general: it must consider *la race, le moment, le milieu*. These conventions have persisted. The point of reference is the past, the subject's period, which must not be rewritten but may eventually be re-evaluated, as Hans Robert Jauss argued. Race would include nationality, not merely broad anthropological categories. Whereas milieux (settings, context) can vary within a lifetime, the time cannot, nor can racial origin. "Determinism," some will cry. Indeed. It does not exclude individual action, however—that is, what we call freedom. Don't I believe in freedom? Yes. But it operates within givens, or "situations," accepting some, using, rejecting, kicking against others, shaping them, acting on them. Pages are devoted here thus to such matters.[2]

According to these nineteenth-century conventions, biographical writing concerning a thinker or creative artist must present both "the man and the work" (or ideas). Like many others, the present memoir often refers to the personal element in light of the literary production, or vice versa. Balzac would approve, as well as Taine, Dickens, Trollope, Zola, Proust, Roger Martin du Gard, and any biographer worth his salt.

---

[2]   Hans-Robert Jauss, *Towards an Aesthetics of Reception* (Minneapolis, MN: University of Minnesota Press, 1992).

Part I

Chapter Two

American Roots: New Utrecht, Ohio, Border South, Colorado

George Eliot wrote that a human life "should be well rooted in some spot of a native land." In France, writing after the amputation of French territory following the Franco-Prussian War, Maurice Barrès urged his compatriots to "root themselves." André Gide, with a Norman mother and a father from the Mediterranean south, inquired where Barrès would want him to take roots. "Où voulez-vous, Monsieur Barrès, que je m'enracine?" That was more than 130 years ago. Imagine the older, heritage Americans in their early days, many challenged by change of language as well as place. Think of more recent arrivals, many from alien cultures. Where are their roots? I think of my mother, partly of New York Dutch ancestry, joined to southern, she herself dying in far Trans-Pecos Texas. The wheel has turned; my daughter now lives quite close to where those Dutch settled. How could these attachments not count for me?

A Teunisse Jansen Lanen Van Pelt (d. 1696), born in Holland and married to a woman named Grietje Jans, emigrated to New Holland in 1663 and the following year built a house, called the Manor House, on a Dutch land-grant plot in New Utrecht (present-day Brooklyn). The house was preserved until the mid-twentieth century. He served as patroon of the village. Their son, Anthony Teunisse Van Pelt, born in Holland, accompanied his parents to New Utrecht. He married

Magdalena Joosten before 1679. Five generations later, through moves to Bucks County, Pennsylvania, and Ohio, Susanna Van Pelt, my direct ancestor, was born (1825).

My mother, née Della Stanforth, held her Dutch heritage dearly but in fact spoke very infrequently of it or other features in her past. She drew her information from a printed Van Pelt genealogy, based on church records of births, marriages, and deaths, as well as civil property records. She had also among her papers sheets typed by a collateral kinsman, with annotated genealogical tables. One note observes that the Van Pelts were a musical line and that the men tended more toward law than medicine. The family may have been originally of the Dutch Reformed Church, but Methodism appears soon in their history. All my background is Protestant, ranging from Methodists to American Baptists to Disciples of Christ to Church of Canada to Episcopalian, with a couple of outliers (Quakers, Christian Scientists).

For some generations, the Van Pelt men tended to marry within what would now be called their community, and the name *Catharine* recurs. Why would they move outside that community? European wars at the time were frequent, usually involving France and the Habsburg empire but often the British and Dutch also. The Netherlands and England were at war repeatedly in the seventeenth and eighteenth centuries. The conflicts spilled over into the New World. In 1664, New Netherland (Manhattan Island) was surrendered to the British, becoming New York. (The Dutch and British did not like each other much in following centuries. Think of the Boer War.)

Other maternal lines include English and Irish surnames. One ancestor was Richard Stanforth, born in Maryland, who settled near Norfolk, Virginia, around 1790. His son James fought in the Battle of New Orleans. His return home, on foot, with scanty supplies and without suitable clothing, through hostile country, left him permanently injured, but he married Esther Shafer, from Augusta County, Virginia. Their son Isaac was born in Lewisburg, Virginia, in 1822. In his early childhood the family moved to a farm four miles south of Hillsboro, Ohio. Isaac married Susanna Van Pelt. Their son, Arthur Gaddis Stanforth (1862-1929), my mother's father, married Susan Wright (1859-1926). Isaac's brother (thus my mother's great-uncle) was a famous Methodist circuit-rider in Ohio, "the Venerable Van Pelt."[1]

The following episode from a sketch of Isaac's life by his brother Commodore B. Stanforth sheds light on the period and the characters I have named. Because Isaac "stood high in the confidence of his community," his signature was accepted as security for a friend's loan. When the friend's business failed, Isaac lost his farm and most of his other property. With what little remained, he went alone to Missouri and purchased unimproved land. Eventually his family could join him. Commodore noted later that "in times of financial reverses, Susanna never complained or found fault."

From Missouri, Mother's ancestors moved to Kansas. It may be Arthur's poor health that took them later to Colorado. Mother spoke of her father occasionally and clearly admired him. He began teaching school in Linn County, Missouri, before he was eighteen years of age. It is said that he had a brilliant mind and was also resourceful, fearless, and quick of comprehension. I recall that she praised his efficiency, and she was proud to show me a letter in which the president of the Gates Rubber Company, in Denver, for which he had worked, commended him in the highest terms. I wish I had known him.

One more line must be traced. A great-grandfather on my mother's maternal side, Thomas Wright, was born in Kentucky in 1799. After his first wife died, he married Sarilda Richardson (1821-1911), who was partly Irish. She was a widow, having wed Joseph Lamberth, with whom she had five children. Her marriage to Thomas Wright produced two daughters, Margaret (1852-1946) and Susan (born in Missouri, 1860, died 1926). Susan became my mother's mother. She lived with the Stanforth family in her old age,

---

[1]   See N. E. Jones, *The Squirrel Hunters of Ohio* (1898; rpt. 2017).

nearly blind. Margaret, known to Mother and me as Aunt Mag, married twice but had no children.

How often wars, in which I take a scholarly as well as human interest, come up in this family's history! An artefact from one in my possession is a walking stick of bois d'arc, or Osage orange, made by a soldier in the circle of Mother's forebears. Having joined the Missouri Mounted Volunteers at the time of the Mexican-American War, he was sent to Santa Fe and El Paso, subsequently to Mexico, where he engaged in the fighting. He carved the stick and took it back to Missouri.[2]

Because of these roots in Virginia and Missouri, a border state, I can claim some southern heritage. My mother's cooking was basically southern—border-southern, I suppose, rather than characteristic of the Deep South. Professor Emeritus Clyde N. Wilson of the University of South Carolina was, I believe, the one who once proclaimed me an honorary southerner. I accept the epithet happily. From age fifteen I have resided in a former Confederate state, and, excepting the University of Nevada Press, all the publishers of my creative work are in the South. Starting with Lewis and Clark, its traditions helped form those of the American west, with which I identify. Similarities between the regions were numerous, even though the west was, for decades, wild and free, without a past (save that of the indigenous peoples), whereas the South had firmly-rooted traditions, which came from England and Scotland and the Common Law, protecting the landowner and even the cotter in his small abode.

Through the heritage of my mother, born in 1895, I am close to an earlier America, which shaped many of her attitudes. Her history will be traced in the next chapter. Here I shall profile three others of her generation who were important to me. (A little boy, Joe, died at birth. I understood that Susan never ceased to mourn him.)

Mother's elder sister, Vera (1886-1981), born in Hutchinson, Kansas, was nine years older but died two years after her. She married a man of excellent character, Raymond Bradshaw. He

---

[2]   See my poem "Osage Orange" in *On the Old Plaza*.

worked principally for the U.S. Forest Service. When I was a girl, he was head ranger of the eastern division of Pike National Forest. The ranger station was located outside Woodland Park, northwest of Colorado Springs. Visits there provided me with a pleasurable and valuable experience of people and mountains. The small house had electricity, generally reliable, but other features suggested an earlier time, including a large iron stove and a wall phone that one cranked to get a party line. I liked the flag ceremonies, in full view of Pike's Peak from the back: raise the flag at morning, lower it at sunset, ceremoniously.

Thomas Jefferson Stanforth (1891-1967), Mother's brother, likewise was born in Hutchison. As a young man he went to Los Angeles. Was he willful? Men are rather expected to launch out, if they feel like it. (Mother herself evinced considerable will, given the time, although she never breached convention.) Tom became an executive of a large confectionary business. He married twice, but had no children. I knew his second wife, from Belfast via Canada, née Kathleen Lindsay, known as Mollie. They were married in Santa Barbara, in a private ceremony, something like an elopement. She is in certain ways the model for "Dora" in two short stories of mine, and she inspired the poem "California, 1936." The title date is wrong if the photos I have were taken on their wedding day, which was in 1937. My mother's notes are not complete. Tom and Mollie drove to visit us in Colorado during many summers. A handsome couple, well dressed, with a suggestion of what was then Hollywood glamor, they were generous to me. A certain thread of eccentricity marked them, though, and there was the matter of Tom's previous divorce; Mother concealed from me that fact and one or two others—perhaps more—during my childhood.[3]

Mother and her sister Margaret, born in 1897, whom I called Margo, were close; Mother suffered in her later decades from living far from her. In the early 1930s, the sisters and Aunt Mag lived in an apartment on Sherman Street near Broadway and First in

---

[3]   The figure in "Dora's Dying" (*An Aesthetic Education and Other Stories*) is modeled roughly on her; the plot is invented.

Denver. It was well located, near numerous businesses, including a millinery shop and the Mayan Theatre, where Margo saw *Gone with the Wind*. (She and Mother spoke about it in hushed tones. Was the "Damn" thrown out by Rhett Butler to blame?) Later Margo and Aunt Mag moved to a tiny house the latter owned on Iliff Street, in South Denver. Unlike my mother, Margo did not drive; she got to work by streetcar number 3. She may have missed Sherman Street and its better shops.

Margo was very attractive. A photograph taken in 1957 shows a slim-waisted woman in a chic dress, self-belted, with her hair (red) stylishly arranged on top of her head. She chose her wardrobe well and could refashion old hats to bring them into style. With some business-school training, she worked for the Denver Department of Welfare, later for the *Rocky Mountain News*, and during long years for Home Services at the Denver branch of the American Red Cross. What are now called "people skills" were her chief asset. She had a warm manner with everyone and was particularly effective on the telephone.

During my girlhood, I knew vaguely of a sometime suitor of Margo's, John Fitzpatrick, a judge, whose mother and sister seemed to be close friends of hers. In recent years I learned from Beth Ann (Coley) Phillips, a first cousin once removed, that Margo had once married a handsome man, apparently a catch, from "back east" (it may have been Milwaukee; she let that name drop sometimes). They left on an eastbound train for their honeymoon. It is said that she returned after a week. That may have been before the romance, if it was one, with John Fitzpatrick. What a story must be there! A diamond ring of hers, handed down in the family, now in the possession of Kate, my daughter, speaks no name.[4]

Nevertheless, Margo was not generally assertive with others. She was amiable, agreeing to their wishes, avoiding censuring them, offering assistance and understanding on all sides. It vexes me to recall how a neighbor, the large, bossy sort of female, quite

---

[4]   See "The Feminist in the Closet" (*The Shimmering Maya and Other Essays*).

uneducated, moreover, treated her. Margo was, to her, "Margaret," but Margo called her "Mrs. Kirby," as though the married state or, more likely, some innate superiority entitled her to that courtesy.

Margo was generous and full of graciousness with me. I remain deeply grateful, and, while she was alive, I had sense enough to show it sometimes. Thus, in the years when I taught on the Atlantic coast, I twice invited her to visit me for a week, paying for her ticket, taking her around to nearby sights that she found enchanting. Doubtless, however, she was wounded by developments in my life, and of course I regret it.[5]

Four or five luxuries she allowed herself. The earliest I know is her Brambach baby grand piano, bought in 1923. She treasured it. Without great skills (perhaps without lessons—I do not know), she played sheet music songs of her early years—"In the Gloaming," "Just a Song at Twilight"—as well as hymns; for years she served as the pianist for the children's Sunday classes at John Collins Methodist Church, conveniently cater-cornered from her. She had the piano shipped to me in the late 1970s. She could no longer play with ease, perhaps owing to arthritis in her fingers. She knew that I would enjoy it and that it would be useful for Kate, who was taking voice lessons. In the aftermath of Katrina—as it stood on soaked carpet and surrounded by dampness for more than five weeks—its ivory keys were ruined, its hammers similarly, and its finish assailed. It required rebuilding and refinishing. It is now prettier than before and still serves me well. Margo gave me also the 1939 Methodist Hymnal to which I allude on occasion.

In later years, when she had more disposable income, Margo's other indulgences were irises, collections of music boxes and expensive costumed dolls, and the stylish clothes she wore so well. A good wardrobe serves the professional woman, of course, but she also had modish and well-made dresses and jackets for evenings. The taste for irises was evident in her large garden, on which she planted beds with various types and hues. She joined an iris society

---

[5]   See "Regret, I" in *Aerosols and Other Poems* on sins of omission and unintended cruelty.

Margaret Stanforth

and attended out-of-state conventions. The irises were left behind when, upon her retirement, she moved to Colorado Springs to be near Vera's family members there.

All my maternal cousins—Ray and Vera's children—were born well before me, three close together before World War I, then a fourth in 1920, and *un petit tardillon* in 1927. During times in Mother's young womanhood when she was in the environs of Colorado Springs, she helped Vera take care of the first three. The eldest, Frances, spent her high school years living in Colorado Springs with her Stanforth grandparents so that she could attend a certified high school (Woodland Park High remained uncertified for long years); she then attended Colorado College. She married a civil engineer and gave birth to a daughter (the aforenamed Beth Ann) even before Mother married. She and three others did well in their careers, two in federal civil service positions, one with the army, a fourth as a banker and administrative judge in Arizona. No enterpreneurs, though. They showed evidence of intelligence and determination.

The life of the second-born, Grace Elizabeth Bradshaw (1913-1993), later Michels, offers a striking example of twentieth-century feminine achievement. It is partly a war story. Trained in Colorado as a surgical nurse, she joined the army as a lieutenant sometime in the early 1940s. Sent to France very shortly after the 1944 Normandy landings, she moved with the Allied forces and remained until 1946, treating the wounded and maimed in field hospital after field hospital. She and Omar Bradley, under whose command she served in the Battle of the Bulge, called each other *Brad*. She had a fiancé, but he was killed in the Far East. After retiring as a major and returning to Colorado, she was told that she could get a medical degree in only two years. She declined the opportunity; she had seen enough blood. Instead, she married and had four children. Her daughter Pat has evinced the same feminine will and intelligence.[6]

In that postwar period, Elizabeth visited us in Denver. She gave me a souvenir handkerchief—another war artefact—made of

---

[6]   See my poem "Lieutenant Fran," in *Breakwater*. Despite the pseudonym, it is a close portrait of Elizabeth.

silk, bearing, in blue embroidery, an outline of Rheims cathedral (badly damaged during World War I and rebuilt in the two following decades—thus a survivor). In one corner, it bears the date "8 mai 1945" (the Germans surrendered to the Allies in a schoolhouse in Rheims on the 7th). How did the French get silk at that period in Europe? I suspect that it was parachute silk. Framed as a diamond, the historic object now hangs diagonally in a bookcase.

Chapter Three

A Portrait of My Mother

Della Leota Stanforth was born on 18 July 1895 in Denver. Why her birth was recorded in Colorado Springs, as she mentioned once, I do not know. The family resided there, west of Monument Creek and the railroad tracks. Beth Ann tells me that the family house was razed during the construction of I-25; I must have driven over the location. The courthouse (El Paso County) having burnt down in 1899, my mother was left without attestation of birth. Upon settling in Alpine, Texas in the late 1940s, she started giving that year, 1899, as her birth date. I view her bit of chiseling as perfectly acceptable. (The story of my parents' moves to Texas will be told in connection with my father, since they were his wish.)

Why did my mother take a different trajectory from those of her sisters? Her aspirations to learning were deep and lifelong. (In the second half of the 1940s, even while running the household and teaching at Colorado Military School, she took and enjoyed a night class on the nineteenth-century American novel. She was not, however, attracted by *Moby Dick*. Not the only one.) She had wished to go to college; she also was drawn to teaching, a genteel calling. At age eighteen, with her diploma from Colorado Springs High School, where she studied both Latin and German, she started teaching school, going by inter-urban streetcar to nearby Fountain. Living at home, she could put money aside. With her savings, she

Della Stanforth upon Graduation from Greeley

enrolled in the State Normal School of Education, in Greeley, now the University of Northern Colorado, and got a bachelor's degree.

She then moved to Wyoming and taught in Torrington and Greybull, where she boarded with respectable families. She spent summers at a dude ranch tutoring a feeble-minded daughter of the owners. (I represented a different challenge.) Mother's sympathies could run deep; she succeeded in teaching her to read and write. I shall note that years later, Mother would tutor in English and history a high school boy stricken with polio and unable to attend school.

Mother returned to Colorado, plausibly because of her parents' poor state of health. Kidney disease afflicted one or both. Her mother died in 1926, her father in 1929. Immediately following his death, their house was robbed before he could be buried; she and Margo had to purchase a suit for the funeral. Not long after, Mother embarked on summer studies toward a master's degree in juvenile psychology at the University of Chicago, where John Dewey had taught earlier in the century. She wrote and typed on a green Royal portable a thesis concerning junior high school adolescents. (For decades I did most of my school, then literary and professorial typing on that handsome machine.) In 1932 she met my father. That story belongs to a subsequent chapter.

I must try to depict my mother's character, going beyond what the preceding paragraphs suggest. She had many virtues, and in her occasional failings she must receive my sympathy. Her steadfastness allowed her to put up with me, obstreperous as I was in insisting on being myself.

Those familiar with the Protestant author André Gide will recognize in her makeup features of his mother, Juliette, and her sister, his aunt Claire Démarest, as depicted in his autobiography, *Si le grain ne meurt* (*If It Die ...*) I have mentioned Gide's Norman roots. The region is known for apples, cheeses, a nutritious, plain cuisine, without spice—and parsimony. The most famous nineteenth-century Norman writers, Flaubert and his pupil Maupassant, are celebrated for detailed descriptions based on facts, not flights of imagination. The area is associated also with the outstanding late nineteenth-century painters who gathered there, but they were generally from elsewhere, not unimaginative Normans.[1]

Gide's family was well established and prosperous. Both mother and domineering aunt, seconded by a Scottish gentlewoman, half companion, half governess, were the soul of practicality and order. They were, however, highly concerned with appearances. Juliette dressed her son in stiff collars, which she considered *de rigueur*, but which he hated; his dislike lasted a lifetime. No suggestion of family penury was admissible; one must, for instance, have a *porte-cochère* (carriage entrance), whether one kept a carriage or not.

Yet ostentation was not permitted either. For a children's costume party, Juliette ruled out anything elaborate on grounds of social tact: one should avoid embarrassing others less well off. She bought for her son the least expensive garb, a pastry cook's outfit. The boy did not want to be a pastry cook. Pirates, knights, Venetian nobles have more style, certainly. André's father, named Paul, was likewise a Protestant but from the South. Despite his eminence as professor of law, he had a poetic inclination (like my father's). Once during the family's twilight walk, he stopped to recite a lyric poem. Juliette admonished him: "Paul, you will recite that when we get home."

To return to Mother's portrait: she was, I have stressed, a nineteenth-century woman. She and countless contemporaries were reared with great emphasis on what a woman *must not do* before marriage, with but little light shed on what she *must do* afterward, lest her husband go to court against her. At least I believe that to be so, prior to World War I. Young women were kept, or kept themselves, in Victorian ignorance. Novels of the period have convinced me that such is not a myth. Doubtless the girls dreaded knowing any details of male anatomy or physiological functions; even if one knew, it must be blocked out as much as possible.

---

[1]   Gide lived from 1869 to 1951. He came from Protestant stock on both sides. The percentage of Protestants in France in 1900 is given as 2%.

Della Stanforth Hill and Catharine Hill

The body cooperated in the endeavor. Desire, if it is to flourish, has to know and understand desire, its own and others'. There was little chance. Mother alluded once, in speaking with me, to those "conjugal duties." If I understand her position correctly, they were to be carried out passively, with affectionate tolerance for the man's special need. She alluded more than once to the great shame that comes upon any family where a girl has been indiscreet—a Jonathan Edwards warning barely updated.

Thus. among my mother's traits, along with concern for appearances, was her extreme prudery. The term *pregnant* was not heard in the household. Having seen a movie in which wild horses appeared, I repeated the word *stallion*. I was told not to use it. To me, it was just a horse. She never mentioned the melodramatic episode in Margo's life. Similarly, she spoke of Tom's divorce only after he was dead. Obliged once to acknowledge an illegitimate child in Vera's circle, she veiled the truth by speaking of a "neighbor's baby." Other relatives shared her attitude. One woman did not learn that her father had been married previously and divorced until the former wife showed up at his funeral.

I never saw Mother cross her legs while seated; her feet were positioned on top of each other. Was that the way prior to 1914? Required seating positions and exact lengths of skirt, on which would depend the amount of stocking visible when a woman sat, entered or left a carriage, or climbed steps, do not interest me much. (Women were taught, I suppose, that men were to precede them in staircases.) What I know is that the position with feet crossed, modest, if you wish, is not attractive. It rules out feminine glamor, the flash of a shapely ankle or calf, the sleekness of a pair of legs, attributes of feminine style emphasized by the movies.

Whether professional or religious, the sense of duty to which so many of her generation were wedded was another strong vein of Mother's character. I have it too, albeit somewhat differently. To what should one be dutiful? Not necessarily what others may think. Her sense of obligation was doubtless inspired by the nineteenth-century imperative, in almost all the nation, to work. ("Let us, then, be up and doing"—Longfellow.) The enlarging United States nation of that century was built on work—both sexes, all races and nationalities, most ages, working assiduously and continually. The leisured—leisured because moneyed—were few in number, though not without influence as providers of work for others. The hymn "Work, for the Night Is Coming" ("when man works no more"), classed thematically under "Activity and Zeal" in my Methodist Hymnal, makes clear that the national imperative had religious as well as moral and economic force. My mother's people were not wealthy and often not even in comfortable circumstances. Her two degrees were thanks to her own industry.

Thus she always had her eyes on the present task, her hands in the kneading bowl or basin, so to speak. She resembled the Charity of Giotto as Proust depicts her—no drama, no proclamation, simply carrying out the work. Wherever we lived, she was an active member of one church or another. She taught adult classes, helped prepare church suppers, visited the aged and housebound, and saw that someone in trouble received assistance. In Texas she was among the founders of the Alpine Community Center (for Mexican-Americans), organized and run by women of the Methodist Church and others. She put benevolence into practice.

It's scarcely necessary to say that she was a careful, though not tyrannical, Dutch housekeeper, in matters of order, cleanliness, meals, and budget. Today I put on my table an old cloth of hers, used for decades, reduced now to utilitarian service, white with embroidered sprigs of heather in the corners. It reminds me of her table settings, always attractive. During her single years, she had been able to acquire plated silverware, Greek key dinner plates, a set of goblets; other attractive pieces must have been wedding gifts.

I recall Mother's efforts, during my junior high school days, to provide me with the required gym shorts. To avoid the expense of purchase, she attempted to make them. Like many women, though not those in my father's family, she knew how to sew on a foot-treadle Singer machine. But she was not skilled. With fabric that may not have been suitable for the purpose, and being obliged to modify a pattern for my skinny frame, she produced a pitiful garment, as she recognized. I wore the shorts nonetheless.

Mother tried to impart to me practical skills. She taught me how to clean a wash basin with a damp cloth and scouring powder. When she took me to a public restroom, she showed me the etiquette to fit whatever arrangement we found. For some reason I remember the powder room (as it was called) on the mezzanine of the Denver Dry Goods Co. Housewives regularly went downtown for everything not available in small neighborhood stores. We would walk four blocks to the number 5 line, ride to Sixteenth Street, and visit "The Denver" or perhaps another department store—Joslin's or, at the other end of the spectrum, Daniel's and Fisher's, the high-end emporium. During an afternoon of shopping, we would visit the powder room, where she guided me.

In short, I commend her for her character—upright in every sense, with moral strength in abundance and the desire to serve others. I thank her not only for her patience and goodness to me during my childhood but also her remunerated employment later, which you will read about, to help pay for my university education.

The trouble was that, while she wanted to help others, I was not simply "another": I was her child, to be formed, if possible. Here I must provide a few indications, to be filled in later, of what I was like in my early years. In some ways I did not need much help, though; in others she thought I would not accept it from her; in the worst case, she may have decided I was beyond help. I am surmising her surmises. None can be entirely wrong. She was handicapped by having a different nature from mine. From a young age, I was a tomboy, with a particular desire to climb trees—an early connection with those marvelous creations. Moreover, I did not care much what others thought. With the exception of the extended family, that is.

Thus I could suggest above that I constituted a "challenge." While Dewey's progressivism may have helped her recognize how much freedom to allow young people, she was not expansive, warm and open—at least not with me. She was not given to silliness, which children love. It may have been her own background that made her somewhat distant. It is certain that effusiveness was less common then than now; people did not hug each other often, I believe, certainly not routinely nor compulsively.

Furthermore, she adhered to the principle that parents and educators were not to coddle children; they must not show too much affection nor convey any sense that the child had unusual abilities. Perhaps she was especially wary about spoiling an only child. She may have patted me on the shoulder on occasion, though, and she sometimes addressed me affectionately by the Dutch nickname *Katrinka*. (My father often called me "Tooner." Aunt Flora used routinely the bizarre "Boolie-Boo," following the "Boolie" that she and others used for my cousin Edith, Uncle Kenneth's younger daughter.)

A final trait of my mother's is her sharp tongue, often censorious. Visiting me when I taught at the University of Florida, and having seen the town a bit, she remarked, "Well, I certainly don't like Gainesville much." Was that a code, meaning "I don't like you much as you are now"? I rather think so. She could not respond warmly to what her constitution—background, training, convictions—disapproved. A few years later, seeing a photograph of a smiling friend of mine with her newborn in a maternity ward, Mother said, "Well, she's certainly not a pretty woman." That comment strikes me as gratuitous; maybe it too reflected some principle.

Oh, poor Mother; she had lost most—not all—of her influence with me and felt it sorely. In 1977, when I told her that the *Sewanee Review*, among the most prestigious American literary publications, had, for the first time, accepted poems of mine, she commented, in an acid tone, "You must have wanted that very badly." Well, of course. As a young woman, she had striven for academic excellence and success in teaching; I strove for the same but literary success also. Earlier I mentioned the prejudice in my milieu against careers on the stage. Poets, especially one who embraced French culture, may have been suspect, at least to her. Did I too speak sharply on occasion? Perhaps, though under my father's guidance I learned, it seems to me, to desist from such phrasings. Others may remember differently.[2]

I feel deeply for Mother in the matter of my father's death. It was devastating. She had supposed she would go first. Perhaps such a prospect gave her pause when she reflected how dependent he was, domestically. But (as readers will see), had he become a widower, he could well have gone off to England and made a bachelor's life there. Instead, she was left, for nearly ten years, to mourn him and blame herself, doubtless, for having rejected a plea for a new, radical move. Additionally, I regret that I was not with her more often. Only twice did Paul Brosman, Kate, and I visit her in Alpine. At least she took the train to see us in New Orleans each Christmastime and occasionally in the spring. One thing that provided enormous pleasure was my gift of a granddaughter for her, an appealing young child.

Mother was not to live past the late 1970s, unfortunately. Twice she was hospitalized during a stay in New Orleans. From the second hospitalization she did not return. Dermatologists whom she had consulted for a persistent rash detected cancer of the cervix. She might have lived with it a year or so, back among her friends, with a doctor she knew well. She did not, I conclude, consider that possibility. Instead, she remained for treatment in an uncongenial city where she knew no one except her small family of three.

Soon the dermatologists arranged for her admission to Touro Infirmary. Oncologists must have been called in, but I met none, ever, and the final bills came from the dermatologists. She underwent countless tests. The medical team decreed that she would be enclosed in a radiation chamber—oh, a small room, I suppose—to be zapped, taken out daily only to undergo further tests, which she was not strong enough to endure. I did not foresee that she would not survive. The evening before her death, I told Kate, then nearly eight years old, to call her grandmother. I can see her now, at the wall phone, speaking sweetly to her and asking her how she was. In that somber box, foreshadowing a coffin, Mother died alone.

---

[2] See "Poem on Striving" in *Aerosols and Other Poems*.

She was given a proper funeral in New Orleans by the vicar of St. Andrew's Church. Two weeks or so later, her friends and admirers in Alpine held another service. Her remains are interred in the wind-whipped cemetery on the south side of the Southern Pacific tracks, overlooked by rickety Italian cypress, quite out of their original landscape. I took the train there to attend the service and close the house. It was sold shortly. On a later visit, I did not drive by to see the property. No matter; the home in my heart remains, to be visited often.

Phoebe Elliott Hill and Edward Hill, 1930s

Chapter Four

American and Canadian Roots: Illinois, Montreal, Colorado

Readers without a historical sense, those who know nothing beyond the current national ethos, will wonder why I do not denounce as bigots or oppressors the forerunners I depict. Many young people denounce theirs, explicitly or implicitly—in print if they are journalists or other writers, or vocally at rallies, protests, and riots, and in acts such as arson, theft, or simply by leaving home without notice for, say, New York, Los Angeles, or Paris, to cast critical light by what they would call their lifestyle on all that past American generations have honored. Obviously, such denunciations go against not only the Decalogue but ages of human experience: we undo what our parents have learned and striven for only at our great peril as well as to our shame. While it is certain that changes in society will come about (though it is hard to foresee which) and, at the present rate, rapidly, there is no ground for presentism. To deplore features of the past—the Inquisition, the Arab and black slave trade, serfdom—is one thing; to condemn today the descendants of human traffickers and all who resemble them is another.

My paternal grandparents were a tremendous presence in my youth and, in memory, remain so. Their tastes, habits, and interests endure in me, whether by genetic or ambient influences. During my first eight years, they resided very near my family in Denver. For the

Mary Beatrice Hill

next seven we were generally just a few miles apart. After the lasting move to Texas in fall 1949, weekly letters kept us in touch, and most summers we returned to Denver for visits. In 1951, when I spent much of the summer living at my uncle Kenneth's house there, the grandparents' home continued to be a pole of my life.[1]

Born in 1863 in Illinois, of caring, generous parents, who took in relatives, Edward Curtis Hill came of New England roots. Four Hill brothers immigrated before 1766. Three returned to England; one stayed. Edward, his descendant, left home as a young man to settle in Colorado, on the western slope. His first job was a lonely one, tending sheep on a ranch some distance from Saguache, the town he chose. When he was able to settle in town, he entered the newspaper business. His brother Albert joined him. For political reasons, their newspaper eventually failed.

At the Methodist church, singing in the choir, he spied in the congregation a young visitor, Phoebe Elliott, and her mother. They became acquainted; the acquaintance then turned into courtship. There must have come a day when he said, "Miss Elliott, may I call you Phoebe?" And she would have replied, 'Yes, Edward, you may." It was she who suggested that he go to medical school in Denver. The three moved there; Edward lived with mother and daughter as a boarder until, once he had received his degree and begun to practice, the young couple was able to marry (May 1893).

A nineteenth-century man who lived through more than half of the twentieth, Grandfather had the eclectic tastes of his period, with the temperament of a scholar and researcher; from him my late cousin Edward, his namesake, an archivist, and I may have inherited the curiosity, patience, and drive that make long hours with a book or historical papers happy ones. Grandfather valued knowledge for its own sake. He read widely and judiciously and bought countless books; he was interested in painting; he listened to recorded music.

---

[1]   See "A House Apart" in *The Shimmering Maya and Other Essays*.

He also loved nature; he dried flowers for albums and collected butterflies, rocks, and photographs. During my university years, he showed interest in my studies and welfare. In the course of his career, he held positions at colleges and on state and national boards. He published books on medicine, including the treatment of pain, and a chemistry textbook (1911), dedicated to "the multitude of students" whom he had taught over many years at the state medical school. I believe, thus, that he knew how to knit social bonds. He enjoyed family society. Even in his extreme old age, he would sit up after dinner in the parlor with the others until he grew too tired.[2]

I must add to this portrait the following illustration of Grandfather's generosity. As a young medical graduate, he first practiced (before settling in Denver) in the foothills to the west. There, he treated without charge a miner from Ohio, Mr. Weber, who lived in a tent with his wife and baby. Their story, the antithesis of the success that Horace Greeley anticipated in saying "Go west, young man," is the basis for my poem "Driftwood." It can be no surprise that the poor man, ill before he settled in that climate or made ill by its rigors in the winter and the altitude, died. The baby died also. Grandfather then assisted the widow, who did not remarry.[3]

In an ironic stroke of fate, she inherited a fortune from her parents in Ohio. Objecting strongly to her marriage, they had disinherited her in favor of another daughter, but upon their death and hers, the family fortune devolved upon Mrs. Weber. She left it all to Grandfather—a large house in East Denver, silverware, fine European furniture, probably shipped to New Orleans and then up the Mississippi and Ohio, eventually overland to Colorado. Three pieces of that furniture and some silverware are now with me. One is a "pier table" dated by a dealer as being from about 1848.

Poems of mine attest to my interest in Fate, called by many names, including, in the Christian mode, Providence. It will be shown

---

[2]   See "Winter Light" in *The Shimmering Maya and Other Essays*, "Four Modes of Book Collecting" in *Music from the Lake and Other Essays*, and "Scarlet Gilia" and its endnote in *On the North Slope*.
[3]   See "Driftwood" in *On the North Slope*.

John Elliott Hill

later that my father was a firm believer in destiny, indeed, a fatalist; maybe the Celts are that way. Chance operates in everyone's life, of course; its workings seem particularly striking in the instance just cited and in my grandmother's case. Witty, sensible, thrifty, devoted to her family, she offered a model for her time and later. She was born in 1864 on Montreal Island and lived there as a girl and young woman. She was Scots-Irish; all her family names that I know are Scottish, including Elliott, from a famous riding clan in Scotland. Their tartan is a beautiful medium blue. The Connells, her mother's line. originated in the Highlands as MacConnells but dropped the *Mac* upon settling in the Lowlands. Her Elliott ancestors arrived in Canada sometime before 1829 from County Clare, in the West of Ireland. Her move to Colorado made possible a long life for her and led to everything written in these memoirs.[4]

Her family was prosperous; her father was in shipping on the St. Lawrence River. In winter, Phoebe, her sister, and her brother skated on the frozen canal to their French-language schools in the city. (There had been other children; but child mortality was high—the rate for all Canada in 1870 is calculated at about 300 per thousand births.) Phoebe's education was, it seems, very solid. Her family owned a piano, and she had musical training. At one time she attended Mount Holyoke College. But she was tubercular, and scarlet fever, rampant, a killer of many, was an additional threat. When she was past twenty, doctors told her mother (her father being deceased) to take her to a better climate, high and dry.

The mother and two daughters took trains to Salida, Colorado, and then a coach to Saguache. Thanks to the dry air, the tubercles in her lungs dried up. Her years were to be long—eighty-eight and a half; but, of slight build, with that history, she was never robust, just morally firm and enduring, thus both weak and strong. In addition to six live births, she suffered three miscarriages. She was given to migraine headaches. (I have been spared those but as a child had

---

[4]   See my thirteen sonnets on fortune, some forthcoming in *Metates and Other Poems,* others in *Fire in the Mind: Poems New and Selected.* Four appeared in *Chronicles: A Magazine of American Culture,* November 2023; others are in print elsewhere.

what I believe to be the sensory disturbances associated with them called *aura*. In my early twenties, it still overtook me sometimes. As I stood by the desk of a research librarian at Rice, listening to his useful tips, I was transported into a sort of second state. It was a strong experience, not erotic in the least. Thinking of the incident—not unique—I suppose it was something in him that called it up. He was a Polish refugee; his experiences in occupied Poland, possibly elsewhere, could have marked him, as with invisible stigmata.)

Phoebe must have missed Montreal terribly at times. She took every child there at least once. It was her home, and she felt loyalty to the Maple Leaf, not the Stars and Stripes. People are attached to their homes. I recall how a man at General Delivery in a small Idaho post office where my parents and I stopped to ask for mail on a long journey to Canada (1966) said, pride radiating from him, "Wherever you're from, you're in God's country now!" Grandmother kept her Canadian ways. She drank tea in great quantities and served it to her children. She had no use for cooking other than her own, especially for foods she considered inferior (ethnic, poor people's diet). She may have missed the sounds of French; though not her mother tongue, she was accustomed to it. Perhaps she and her eldest child (Mary Beatrice, 1894-1986), who studied in Montreal, conversed in it. (My devotion to that language does not, however, spring from the family.) Because of Grandmother—and a summer term teaching in her homeland—I have a strong sentimental attachment to it.

Her Scots-Irish brogue marked not only her but also her children, and a bit lingers with me. A school official who interviewed my father for a teaching position told him that to be hired in his district he would need to take elocution lessons. During the frequent singing sessions in my grandparents' house, Scottish songs were especially honored, and Grandmother used time-honored expressions: "A bonny face is easily decked"; "Many a mickle makes a muckle"; "There's many a slip 'twixt the cup and the lip."

She had a strong sense of independence and a tremendous will. She also had her own bank account (family money), with which she purchased the mountain cabin near Bailey that furnishes the setting for one of my poems reflecting on war. Yet the early years of marriage, as Grandfather built his medical practice and children came, cannot have been easy for either spouse. Mary was obliged to help in the household; Flora (1900-1986), who will get her own chapter in this narrative, was ill for long years.

In time, Grandmother's routine was eased. In my childhood, at least, she had a washing woman, a Mrs. Kenyon; in later years, it was a Mrs. McCullough. The Irish so often have worked, and worked hard, for others. Grandmother's home was well ordered and gracious, with lovely furnishings, including oriental carpets; but today's vulgar, hedonistic displays were unknown. Often, she bought the best products available, preferably imported from Great Britain: tea, biscuits, marmalade, mint jelly for lamb. This was not a snobbish habit; she was not a foodie, nor was she moved by advertisements. It's that she recognized differences in quality, which she had learned, doubtless, in her own mother's home.

During my childhood, Phoebe had a dog, Chang, a chow, which I was told not to touch. "He does not like children." Warning enough. Chang remained under others' care when Grandmother went traveling, but he was essentially her dog. Generally obedient, he was beside himself when the family went into the foothills for a drive or picnic; many meadows there (not yet filled in by exurbs) had herds of cattle, at which he barked vigorously. No eloquence could make him desist—only a bend in the road.

In certain respects, Grandfather, doubtless with Grandmother's concurrence, departed significantly from the model of the nine-teenth-century patriarch. He put their two daughters as well as all four sons through the University of Denver, to which they took streetcar number 8. At one time or another, all six pursued further studies. Mary took summer graduate courses at Boulder (University of Colorado) and studied piano in France; Flora took a degree at the University of Michigan. Those two had great confidence in themselves, it seems to me. Both drove (the garage had been converted for a motor car).

Presumably, Grandfather expected his sons to follow professions that he deemed worthwhile. Frederic Henry, the eldest (1896-1954), studied chemistry and worked in that industry in San Bruno, California. Might Grandfather have preferred medicine for him? Kenneth Alfred (1898-1973) became a physician and surgeon; together, father and son later ran Hill Laboratories in Denver. Kenneth was the father of my older cousins John, Jean, and Edith, who were present in my girlhood and played a role in my retirement years.

Jack (John Elliott, 1902-1944), having graduated from law school at the University of Denver, hung out his shingle. He had an appealing personality. But the poor man was unsuited for practice, being without aggressive instincts and more likely to reconcile parties than represent one against the other. Nor was the Depression a favorable time; he would assist clients but not get paid. He failed. At some date he went to Seattle, where work was available. It was not the right work. Having signed on as a strike-breaker, he was beaten viciously by anti-scab union members—so badly that only skin grafts done by Kenneth, who arrived by train, saved his life. Did Jack have a roaming instinct? In Albuquerque, he started a business, Hill Truck Line, and married a woman named Thelma, whose sister he had courted earlier, unsuccessfully. Ultimately, he joined the Navy as an able-bodied seaman, dying at the Battle of Leyte Gulf. A letter in my father's handwriting, postmarked the 27th of September 1944, was returned by the Fleet Post Office Directory Service as undeliverable.[5]

According to what I once heard, the fourth son, Paul Victor, my father (1907-1969), who will receive a full portrait in the following chapter, was expected, or urged, to go into dentistry. Nothing came of that; I suspect he simply did not want to be a dentist.

I have indicated that Grandmother returned by train to Montreal from time to time. After Grandfather's retirement in 1933, the two traveled abroad extensively. In papers held by my cousin Charlie Hill, there are allusions to multiple voyages, including one around the

---

[5]   See www.findagrave.com/memorial and various poems, including "Phoebe 1944" in *Arm and Arm*.

world, a trip up the Amazon, traveling to Alaska, crossing the Arctic Circle, and seeing the Northern Lights. Dates and itineraries are often unclear; there are attestations for others. One is a turquoise bracelet I have that, according to my understanding, was bought for Mother in Peru. By the way, I am not the only descendant who evinces a similar determination to travel. When Jean and her husband, Dwight Miller, had reared their children and their businesses had prospered, they drove and flew his plane around the Four Corners states; they also crossed the Atlantic to Scotland, the home of multiple ancestors. Jean visited their son James in Borneo, and she and James went hiking and camping in Patagonia and the Dolomites.

A small leather-bound daily logbook of Grandmother's, with an attached pencil, called "Travels Abroad," documents certain voyages in detail. A sticker identifies it as having come from Daniel's & Fisher's, which had a stationery counter as well as a good book section. I take delight in the fidelity with which she kept records on shipboard. (For me the nearest testimonies are my two series of poems on voyages around South America and a third on a cruise to Singapore.) The little diary opens with a trove of information. Pages in color show national flags, "funnel and house flags," pilot flags and banners; tables of distances; notes on money and passports; customs regulations; shipboard information; and wardrobe suggestions for both sexes.[6]

The list is slanted toward shipboard life, but train accessories are mentioned also. "Traveling Necessities for Women" suggests "simple frocks" of chiffon for afternoons and two "smart evening gowns," a short evening wrap, preferably in black velvet, a sports coat of camel hair or tweed, turbans or berets, and, for cold foreign hotels, hot water bottles. Pullman slippers are mentioned for the train. Grandmother surely had a pair. Women did not roll all this through airports and place it on scales themselves; porters were everywhere. Steamer trunks were loaded into the baggage car of the train, carried on board the ship, unpacked, and then stored below decks. Sturdy satchels served as personal luggage. What

---

[6]   See *On the Old Plaza* and *A Memory of Manaus*.

finery Grandmother packed I do not know. She would have dressed properly, always. A passport picture of the 1930s, set in a little frame with my grandfather's, shows a serious, frank-eyed woman, dressed in a dark color but with a blue scarf at her throat.

In 1938 they crossed the Atlantic on *The City of Hamburg*, a mail ship, and continued their journey by a circumnavigation of Africa, followed by a recrossing westward. The first journal entry, on December 14th, shows they were in London, "cold and damp"; on the 23rd, in Las Palmas (Canary Islands); subsequently they stopped at Ascension Island and St. Helena, where Grandmother pronounced the weather to be perfect. Cape Town was "extremely hot." as was Zanzibar. Such names as Aden, Arabia, Port Sudan, Suez, Cairo, and Port Said dot her next pages. The ship then called at Genoa, Tangiers, and Gibraltar. She must have welcomed British territory again. Unfortunately, pages that may refer to other Italian stops are illegible, the pencil marks having grown too faint.

That voyage, that time seem very distant to me now. For America, it was peacetime, though a shaky peace. Less distant is September 1939, when the war on which I have written poems and prose broke out. The grandparents were in Colorado, but Aunt Mary was in France, studying piano at the Fontainebleau Conservatory. The Mediterranean and Atlantic were no longer safe for pleasure travel; the promise of "Peace in Our Time" had fallen apart; Europe was changed, drastically. She got to America with difficulty.

Yet there was time for one last, long voyage, to Japan. Few imagined that the Asiatic wars of the time would involve before long the rest of the world. My grandparents sailed on the *Nitta Maru* from San Francisco in June 1940. Grandfather sent me a postcard written on board. It shows a hibiscus flower in Hawaii. I do not remember their departure but have some vague image of their return, as they distributed gifts among us. The little silk kimono they brought for me is gone, but I have my parents' gifts, a set of silver coffee spoons with Japanese motifs and a painted fan with wide ribs of genuine ivory, displayed with other Asian objects on my piano. A note in Grandmother's diary surprises me: in Honolulu she ate at a Chinese restaurant. I would not have thought it possible. Perhaps I do her an injustice in attributing to her narrow tastes in food.

Both Grandmother and Grandfather appreciated the Rockies enormously. She shared his interest in botany; Grandmother's travel journals abroad mention flowers and trees she had seen, and I have noted that Grandfather pressed leaves and blossoms for albums. (His collecting did not harm any species.) Short day trips to the mountains, maybe just a picnic in the foothills, were frequent. Wyoming was an attractive destination for them. When Grandfather was a widower, he was pleased when Aunt Flora could drive him there. (In Wyoming, one can get to spectacular mountains with less risk to the heart by avoiding the dangerously high elevations of Colorado's Front Range.) I have a postcard from him, showing Loch Vale, a gorgeous sight, dated summer 1953, mentioning a trip with the aunts through Estes Park on to Wyoming. He signed it, "Success and happiness, Grandfather."

When Grandmother died of cancer, shortly before New Year's, 1952, my father was with her; learning that she was in her last days, he had taken the train from Alpine to El Paso, thence to Albuquerque, thence to Denver, sitting up all the way because no berth or roomette was available. She was buried in Fairmont Cemetery, where Aunt Mary's remains later joined hers. When Grandfather, enfeebled, died, more than five years later, his old heart finally unable to continue beating, I was in France. According to his wishes, he was cremated. Aunt Flora imparted the news to me by letter: "We will all miss our loving Father and Grandfather."

Chapter Five

A Portrait of My Father, with Mother and Me

Sometimes I think I owe my father, Paul (1907–1969), almost everything; he cast on my life not a long shadow but long beams of light. I called him "Daddy" or, sometimes, "Papacito"—when Mother became "Mamacita"—but those names cannot be carried over into this account. I have paid homage to him again and again, in prose, poems, book dedications, and conversations. Always, when speaking of him, I add, lest there be misunderstanding, that he was a very fine man and nothing I say is to be taken as a reproach. If ever he is to incur any blame, it will not be from me. As my poem "An Epitaph for My Parents' Graves" says, "That which they did was well done." He exemplified prudence in its fullest sense: cultivation of the good and avoidance of the harmful—the seven deadly sins and their modern equivalents. I summed up his gifts in a dedication as "measure and light."[1]

My parents met in autumn 1932, when my father was studying for a teaching certificate and was assigned to practice teaching with a Miss Stanforth, at Grant Junior High School. I can come no closer now than before to elucidating the exact circumstances.

---

[1]   For the dedication, see *Journeying from Canyon de Chelly*. For the poem, see *A Memory of Manaus*.

Paul Hill in His Classroom, 1930s

Who was this young man who entered Mother's classroom? The last-born of his family, he was the only one to attend a public elementary school. (The older children had been tutored at home, then sent to private schools.) As a boy, he was fond of the King Arthur tales. He was good-looking, slim and muscular, and liked sports as practiced then. He was, I have reason to believe, well liked. His bachelor's studies at the University of Denver included political science and Spanish. He did not begin his college work there, however, but at Northwestern University in greater Chicago, where his brother Kenneth studied medicine and did his internship. Unlike Kenneth, my father did not like what he found there. It was the climate, doubtless. He never liked cold weather, I have concluded, and suffered from it. What else? Had Grandfather pressed him to go, perhaps because a change seemed advisable, or because Kenneth was there? At any event, my father returned to Denver, after a year, I suppose.

Almost everything about his life in the mid to late 1920s and early 30s is murky to me. A few textbooks of his on my shelves reveal, at least, some of what he read, including histories of Rome and England. I do not know the date of his bachelor's degree. Having worked in a drugstore, he wanted to open one, with a soda fountain. (He owned a malted milk machine.) The drugstore project seems to have been abandoned; Grandfather discouraged it, as I read in a letter dated 1932 on stationery from the St. Anthony Hotel in San Antonio, where my grandparents had stopped on their travels. The letter concerned Father's plan to marry and his situation. Grandfather, knowing the times and my father's character, warned him, noting that there were already two drugstores near the location Father had in mind; moreover, "the Hills have never been good in business." At what must be a later juncture, my father owned a grocery store. I *may* remember visiting the modest place; I recall talk about it.

Then what was he doing in 1932 preparing to be a teacher? Perhaps his practice-teaching was not part of a full-time curriculum; it may have been an interim step, a sort of insurance policy. Or maybe

Della, Paul, and Catharine Hill

the plans for a business looked shaky. Anyhow, he was assigned to Mother's classroom. The two were engaged by December and married the following June. My great-aunt Mag's name was on the invitation as the remaining member of her parents' generation.

The families were doubtless happy with the match. In his letter from San Antonio, Grandfather wrote to Father: "Della is a very fine woman." Quite so. One wonders, though, if the age difference, easily noted, bothered some observers. Margo, kind and giving of herself, must have rejoiced that Mother had met a man worthy of her. But Margo was left alone to care for Aunt Mag, who could do a great deal for herself and the household but not everything. Margo's salary at the Department of Welfare was very low, and for some months it was not paid at all nor made up later. The women must have been on a very tight budget.

My parents' wedding trip took them, as I understand it, to the old Antlers' Hotel in Colorado Springs then to Grand Lake. Father evoked the time occasionally: "Della, do you remember ... ?" Mother owned a red Chevrolet. It was she who taught my father to drive. Previously, she and her car had been in an accident on the old highway from Denver to Colorado Springs. (That was two highways before the current I-25.) The car had rolled over; her nerves were sorely tried. I don't know who was at the wheel for the honeymoon.

Given Mother's age and the economic conditions as well as my father's uncertain health (to be discussed later), might they have preferred to remain a childless couple? An off-hand comment Mother made when I myself was pregnant invites me to conclude so: "Well, you will want that child when it comes." She was speaking for herself, perhaps; I was happy all along, certainly. I recall how one day when Paul, Kate's father, and I were walking along Panola Street, in his neighborhood, we talked about having a little heir. Mother had made a point once of saying to me, sounding resigned, that parents "must be responsible for those whom they bring into the world." Both my parents loved me, I am confident.

They got me, anyway. And I count myself very fortunate to be the daughter of that couple and to have lived around other adults of high character and intellect, who helped them with me on occasion and, surely, contributed to making me.

After my parents married, they lived for more than a year in an apartment on York Street at East Colfax. With money Grandfather had bestowed on my father at his majority, as he had done for the others (I believe it was $5000, a handsome sum at the time), they bought a bungalow built a few years earlier (the house was sold in 1949), on South Race Street, a mile or so from my grandparents' house on East Alameda. When I was five, they leased it so that they could rent a corner house not many blocks away but very close to an elementary school, Washington Park, to which I could walk by myself; the previous district school was judged too far. It is to the honor of the canine race that my dog, Beans, acquired when I was quite small, probably to provide companionship for the only child, understood that in the afternoons he might sit at the corner, on our property, waiting for me to return from school, but must not rush ahead to meet me.

Of the kindergarten teacher, a Mrs. Nielson, my mother observed that she could not distinguish between *bring* and *take* and consequently misused the former regularly. "Now bring this home with you," she would say to children departing for the day. Poor Mrs. Nielson! She was censured (privately, of course) for a fault that, in our present time, is so widespread that journalists writing for the *Wall Street Journal* make it commonly. (I subscribe to that sheet not for business reports but general news from America and Europe and, particularly, the daily book reviews and art, architecture, and film articles.) Do I get from my mother the instinct of a grammarian and word specialist—as in *Fowler's English Usage*—allowing me to spot and correct such errors? Presumably. As students and a few acquaintances will attest, I've got it, one way or the other.

The neighborhood of that elementary school was central to my young life, although we returned, after an interval in an apartment, to the original house. The Brownie, then Girl Scout troop to which I belonged for seven years was composed of pupils from Washington Park, and later I attended a community Protestant church there, associated loosely with the Methodists, which served many families and young people.

I have explained that I was never told I was unusual, although once my mother did let out the fact that as a small child I had done very well on the Seashore Measures of Musical Talent. Results of an IQ test, probably at school, were not imparted to me. Finally, when I was about to go to The Rice Institute, my father observed to me, while we were alone, that I was highly intelligent. (In France, Roger Martin du Gard and his wife took, for their daughter, Christine, the same approach: impart no sense that the child is not like all others in their milieu.)

After our return to the bungalow, the remainder of my early schooling, except the year one year away, took place at Steele Elementary School, where my father had gone, probably from its opening in 1913. From Steele I can remember one teacher's name—Miss Armitstead; she boarded with us. And I have not forgotten Mrs. Diehl, the music teacher from grade three on, who taught us to spell her name, then that of Tchaikowski, to whose music she introduced us. She was also my first flute teacher. Names of pupils come back to me—Janie Watkins; Mary Bullock, who lived not far from my grandparents' house and with whom I sometimes walked at the end of the school day; and John and Jane Hall, neighbors, two doors away. John was a classmate and pal through nearly all my Denver schooling. Jane was two years younger. A boy named Bill Barlow is still in my recollections; he was disobedient, frequently—the only example of such I can recall.

My mother was friendly with John and Jane's mother and, after our definite departure from Denver, the two women stayed in touch. Time brought an end to their correspondence. Three years ago, Jane, looking through an address book of her mother's, found my name, Brosman, the note "Della Hill's daughter," and an address in New Orleans. Looking me up, she got my email address and wrote to me. The result was a long telephone call from Hawaii, where John lives in retirement from his position as professor of biochemistry at the University of Hawaii. He taught there for decades but spent considerable time elsewhere for professional and personal reasons. A hiker as a boy, he became an authority on Hawaii trails and wrote a book on local trailside flora.

We all met subsequently in Olathe, Kansas, while John was visiting his sister and her husband, Dick. What an interesting reconnection! We exchanged photos of our common past, showing front porches, my dog, and the three of us out in the snow. John and I evoked games we played inside, including a huge board game we created from a wide box-top, with an imaginary geography and multiple routes and choices. Our lives, with their travels, turned out to be somewhat like that board game.

Father taught in the year 1933-1934 but was, perhaps, involved also in the grocery business. Mother had been obliged to resign from the Denver schools because of a policy forbidding employing spouses. It was she who left, of course. A self-respecting man could not agree to being what westerners called a "squaw man." But she would have had to leave anyhow because she was expecting me, and a visibly pregnant woman, as she would be, could not appear in a classroom. Thus, my father learned that, as the proverb has it, "He who has wife and child has given hostages to Fortune." Indeed, but he could not have regretted his marriage nor my birth. Nothing but loss came from the grocery venture, I believe. Anyway, teaching turned out to be his lifetime calling.

Father was exceptional in more than one way. Marrying a woman older than he by more than eleven years was unusual, certainly. In a photograph of the two taken probably in 1935, she is slim and looks younger than in a studio portrait of not many years later (I may have contributed to her aging); but the difference in years could not go unnoticed, especially since her hair turned gray quite early. She was very intelligent, more than he, as he asserted when I was sixteen. (That acknowledgment shows how different he was from most of his sex.) Her mind and character, not superficial, must have been huge attractions. If not dazzling beauty, she had distinguished looks, her intelligence visible.

My parents never addressed before me the matter of their marriage. But once my mother volunteered her view that my father could not have married a young, silly thing, nor any woman markedly inferior to him, in tastes and intellect, as were, doubtless, most of those he met, even at the university. He needed, moreover, a particular dimension of understanding, one nurtured by experience and with a stellar character. Let us say that he had a tender sensibility. He saw it in me likewise, and tried to protect me, while recognizing that one needs to develop at least a bit of resistance and toughness. "Into each life some rain must fall; some days must be dark and dreary." I recall those words with some shame, realizing that the frequency with which he quoted them suggests that he heard a few too many complaints.

As a boy, my father would have attended services at whatever Protestant church Grandmother chose, perhaps a Methodist congregation, perhaps Central Presbyterian, which she frequented later. He must have been present at evangelical or revivalist services at some time. He spoke derisively of a preacher who, when the collection plate was passed, called out, "Folding money, boys, only folding money." At no time in my life did he accompany Mother to any of the various Protestant churches to which she belonged. Some observers may have considered him a lost soul, literally, others supposing, with some reason, that it was his dislike of entanglements or his need to conserve his strength.

Father had enjoyed summer weeks at Camp Chief Ouray, in the Estes Park area then, now near Granby. I believe that he and Jack both worked there subsequently. Perhaps his good experiences led him to understand why I would take right away, at age eleven, to the Flying-G Ranch, a Girl Scout camp. Both were Christian, explicitly or otherwise, with provisions made for services on Sunday. Was it at Chief Ouray that he learned such hymns, which he sang often, as

"Brightly Beams Our Father's Mercy"? It is included in a 1938 edition of the *Cokesbury Worship Hymnal*, which my friend Joseph Warner gave me. I do not find there, however, another favorite of my father's, "The Railway to Heaven," which seems to date from the 1890s.

A third hymn in his repertory, "Higher Ground" (1926), furnished the title of an essay collection of mine.

I'm pressing on the upward way;

New heights I'm gaining every day;

Still praying as I'm onward bound,

"Lord, plant my feet on higher ground."

The Protestant imperative for self-improvement—the same imperative expressed in my mother's adages and certain hymns she liked—and the American drive toward progress join here in a national vision akin to that of Katherine Lee Bates in her famous song while drawing on the biblical tradition of mountaintops. The title essay gives to the movement upward a literal, topographical meaning—driving into Colorado—but stresses that any moral improvement we can bring about must, at best, be very slow.

Father's position on the Church of Rome is worth noting. As a youth or young adult, he may have had encounters with Catholics, and from his study of European history and general reading he would have gained considerable knowledge. It inspired in him dislike and fear, which he considered well founded, in view of both the past and his own time, when the popes had not yet abandoned their claim to exclusive control of salvation. It is too easily forgotten that Catholics were forbidden to attend services of any other religious body. My father knew of priests who forbade their parishioners, explicitly, to consult a Bible. In his view, those positions were obscurantist. I share his dislike, if not the fear; my Catholic friends will need to forgive me—as they and others must for other failings that I don't have the wits or moral depth to perceive.

My father was a thrifty man. Thrift was instilled in him by his mother and generations of Scots behind her; it was also the default style of living for the majority in America then, whether urban or rural. He and Mother must have been like my former apartment-mate at what was then The Rice Institute, Evelyn (Powell) Payne, as loyal a friend as one can have, who said of herself and her husband, "Both misers." When, however, it came to what my father valued most, he put money on the table. He and Mother did well by me. I have just mentioned Scout camp; I also had private music lessons and attended a superior university. He would have gone to almost any length to make that possible. In time, they were able to spend money on their own adventures.

My father's intellectual loves were the English language and British and Anglo-Irish literature, especially poetry. He must have studied the latter in college, but he would have been familiar with English-language verse already from his parents' conversation and his father's library. Teaching English, he concluded, was less onerous than other ways to earn a salary. His devotion to the subject would have inspired students. The pay was low, to be sure, so low that summer after summer he had to make extra money, once by running a boys' camp, some summers and on many Saturdays by giving drivers' examinations or doing safety demonstrations to truckers at the State Fair in Pueblo. Even after the permanent move to Texas, he returned to Colorado for a whole summer's work.

Father was not, however, a well man. Grandmother was more than forty-two when he was born. He probably had bad lungs from birth. He was terribly susceptible to upper-respiratory infections. He had little physical endurance; he needed rest. I recall how, when he returned from teaching at North High School, in a distant neighborhood he did not like, he would stretch out to rest on a studio couch in our small dining room. He often directed barbs at the principal and the school superintendent, a Mr. Green, for pedagogical transgressions—introducing sex education was one—but even more, I think, for assigning him to North in the first place. South High, a good school, not far from us, or East High, where his friend Arnold Ward taught and located in a better neighborhood than North, would have been more practical for him, and his talents would have gone farther. He joked about wishing to address to the school offices boxes containing "gifts" such as toads and roaches.

My father's ability to take things philosophically was on display frequently. Human beings cannot forget the morrow, or do so at their expense. But to seize the day and live it in contentment, if possible, is wisdom. His sunny disposition was a gift to others and an example to me. Was he not miserable inside, though, full of melancholy, black bile? Doubtless. He would sit silently with his head in his hands. One did not disturb him then. I suffer much less from melancholy; but some comes out in wintertime, during gray, cold, dreary days. Many poems of mine concerning the American southwest, with its powerful sun shining on red and yellow stone, were composed as an escape in wintertime. What would I do in Sweden or Alaska?

In *Huis-clos* (*No Exit*), Sartre showed how, in human relations, three is a difficult number; it's usually two against one. Perhaps. Sartre could have experienced it through his numerous liaisons, in which Beauvoir was one of the triangle, left out often, doubtless. Or the conviction could have arisen in Sartre's childhood: his widowed mother and he lived with his grandparents, who called them "les enfants"—thus reducing two generations to one and producing a triangle, with an authoritarian patriarch having a monopoly and a second-fiddle grandmother, the forces playing off against one another.

My family's dynamics contravened that pattern often. We played board games and Anagrams (a forerunner of Scrabble). I recall the three of us seated on a sofa when I was little, talking and laughing merrily in a three-way bond. Sometimes we acted out a "Yukon game," wrapped under the afghan Grandmother had made for her son and pretending that we were on a sled of some sort. "Mush, mush!" Father would call to the imaginary dogs. "On to Dawson!" He would have avoided taking my side in my overt disputes with the one responsible for everyday discipline; wise parents make common cause. But a special father-daughter bond was there and flourished.

A photograph from my early twenties shows my father and me on the family couch, smiling and laughing together. It is eloquent. We were "les enfants."[2]

Practicality, the imperative for most women, means attending to the present. Men, in contrast, may see farther and particularly take a wider, even loftier view. Prehistory shows that men roamed farther afield, pursuing game (or making war on other tribes), while the women were at home in the cave or hut, tending the fire and the offspring. One has only to study the mores and records of the Oklahoma Kiowas in the nineteenth and early twentieth centuries, as recorded by them and others, to see a modern example of this arrangement—an illustration of the "vertical" versus "horizontal" distinction between the sexes of which feminists make much. (Some take pride in it; some blame men for imposing it.)[3]

Father sensed, of course, that the prudent husband generally yields to his wife's superior wisdom or at least her preferences. My daughter, Kate, was once asked whether she and her husband, Brian, although very happily married, as all can see, had occasional disagreements. "Oh, yes," she replied, smiling, "but I always make him see the light." Indeed. Be it understood that I hold my son-in-law in high regard—as of course she does also; hence the smile. From the beginning of their marriage, in 1997, she has been an excellent wife, then mother, and "domestic engineer," whether teaching at Columbia or elsewhere, employed by an art magazine, or as now, working as a certified translator from French.

My mother must have had her way, thus, in many things. For instance, in Denver my father had to endure visits from "charity couples" whom, in her goodness, she succored modestly during the Depression, and from the minister at her church, who called him "Professor"—an inflated title, probably embarrassing. There, and later in Texas, it was she, I believe, who decided who would be invited into their home. If memory serves, though Mother was friendly with

---

[2]   See the poem "Afghan," in *Arm in Arm*.
[3]   See the chapter on Alice Marriott in my book *Southwestern Women Writers and the Vision of Goodness.*

several neighborhood women, including Mrs. Loring, the wife of a Jewish Army Air Corps captain, the only neighbors invited to visit were the Olivers, next door. A colleague of my father's at North High School and his wife exchanged visits with my parents, but I believe that another friend of his at the school was not invited. No wife? Or unacceptable wife? Mother's girlhood friend Esther Stanton and her husband Elmo visited us, and we went to their house. They had a daughter in her early adulthood, married. I recall my father suggesting that the man she'd chosen was not of much account—a rare, significant censure from his lips.

As you would expect from her portrait earlier, Mother generally carried out her domestic functions well, avoiding giving my father foods he did not like and adhering carefully to the family guidelines for expenditures and routines. I have mentioned, however, her sharp tongue, from which my father suffered sometimes. His parents had given her a beautiful bowl from the Moorcroft pottery in England. Alas, he broke it. The incident was recalled often, embarrassingly so.

Then there was the matter of the second-hand piano purchased by my grandmother as a gift for him and delivered to the house, but without forewarning. It arrived while he was absent—an unwelcome surprise to Mother, dusty, I recall her complaining, perhaps not very attractive. Mother ordered it sent back. What each spouse said to the other in private, and how my father explained the refusal to his mother, I do not know. But the episode remains in my mind. My father played by ear; he enjoyed doing so. The piano could have been dusted and covered partly with a drapery of some sort. Or, carried down the back staircase, straight, to the basement, it could have fit well into the finished den, a bit cool perhaps in the winter (the only heat coming from a small space heater, to be used sparingly) but pleasant otherwise. I cannot imagine how Mother could have refused the instrument.[4]

Nor did she take into consideration the advantage for me of having a piano at home; my practice was on the Steinway belonging to my aunt Mary, who was my teacher, and Margo's baby grand, stored

[4] See "Sarabande" *On the North Slope.*

with us for a short time only. (It now stands in my main room.) What if, later, I had wished to major in music, or at least have a minor? Because of my good performances on the flute in high school, I was awarded a music scholarship to Texas Western University (ex-Texas School of Mines, now UTEP). From what I understand, however, I would have been disadvantaged by not having a better command of the keyboard. Oh, Mother could not see that far ahead. I must forgive her, of course, and I do.

Although mild of manner, the least tyrannical of men, but deeply needy, Father was the agent for the most important household decisions. He asked a great deal of Mother, not routinely, but at crucial times, and she recognized when she must yield. He took two leaves of absence from North High School in search of a warmer climate; he suffered from cold weather. The first was in 1943, for part of a term which he spent in Arizona. Mother and I stayed behind in Denver for some weeks but then joined him, traveling on the Santa Fe railroad via Albuquerque, where we spent a night between trains at a Harvey House hostelry. I have recounted elsewhere how, sleepwalking, I left the hotel room and went along the corridor and, I believe, downstairs.

In August 1944 my parents embarked on a lengthier enterprise. They rented out the house and left by car, angling down across New Mexico to the Panhandle of Texas, then farther, in a southeasterly direction. Given wartime restrictions on speeds, the trip took ten days. In my essay on the adventure, I called it "the shimmering maya"—the veil of illusion.[5]

When they reached warmer latitudes, they stopped in small towns where Mother might find a still-unfilled high school teaching position. In Edinburg, she was hired for social studies, I think. My father somehow got a job as circulation manager at the daily newspaper, which served several towns right by the Rio Grande. With so many men in the armed forces, male employees were hard to get; I suppose that the management wanted a man for

---

[5]   See the title essay in *The Shimmering Maya and Other Essays.*

the job. He was to drive the citrus groves to get new business. His personality was what is called "winning." Still, I don't know how many subscriptions he sold.

The stay in Edinburg lasted only for that school year. Why did we not stay? Father thought the climate, benign by its mildness, was probably insalubrious in other ways—yellow fever, perhaps. He may have missed the Denver family. Jack was killed that fall. When news of his death reached us, after some weeks, a dark veil fell over everything. The return to Denver brought some consolation, surely; one wants to mourn with others, not in solitude. How painful his reflections were, each time he reflected anew that, as Kenneth wrote, the family "would never see Jack's smile again, nor hear his voice."

The two stays, in Arizona and Texas, may have done Father some good, but their benefit was not lasting. In October 1949, he suddenly quit his teaching job at North High (but after what mental agitation?) and told Mother they must put the house up for sale. Before long, we were gone, headed for Alpine, in Trans-Pecos Texas. My mother, trooper as she was, saw that she must agree to move, for the greater good.

Are you surprised that I was not consulted about that change? Parents did not inquire of teen-aged children whether they approved of family policy. Nor did it occur to me to protest. "What about your friends?" someone asked. I did not mind, really; anyway, if she could take it, couldn't I also?

Retrospectively, I might regret having missed further adventures at the Flying-G; I am sorry that I had to leave the chorus and orchestra of South High School and give up the chance to start Latin the following year. Lessons with Aunt Mary on her Steinway and flute and theory lessons with an accomplished flautist would never be resumed. Those doors had closed; others would open.

One must understand that my father did not change jobs or locations for reasons of ambition; he had next to none. Meeting my mother in that classroom had doubtless injected him once with a new vitality; marrying her meant responsibilities, and he took them seriously, always. But he was a restless man, and remained so. How can I not understand him? I likewise am restless. Ah, the wisdom of Descartes (and Alcoholics Anonymous, I believe): since you cannot change the world, act on yourself. Such a wise path! So hard to follow!

Alpine, the seat of Brewster County in Trans-Pecos Texas, at nearly 5000 feet of elevation, surrounded by arid mountains and rangelands, may be viewed as forlorn and unappealing. Like Marfa, about twenty-five miles away, even Ft. Davis, which is higher and has a running creek, Alpine and the vast, dry stretches surrounding it were not meant by God to be fashionable. There's little water; creek beds are dry, usually. Trees are sparse in many places; the soil is stony. Huge hot springs in Balmorhea, north of Ft. Davis, demonstrate what's in the aquifer below; but in most of the range, one must dig way down to reach it. Unfortunately, like neighboring counties, Brewster has become a popular, almost exotic destination. Human folly and greed, fed by the excess of money these days, have damaged the surroundings by scandalously using up water, confining animals in enclosed parks where hunters (not "sportsmen") pick them off easily, and establishing leisure spots and horrid "art" installations. "It's art if you think it is," pronounced the late Donald Judd, responsible for one of those eyesores, which consists of a hundred aluminum sculptures, glorifying the ego but disfiguring the landscape.

We had a lovely autumn trip down through New Mexico, partly along the Pecos River, where golden cottonwoods were kings' treasuries. Before reaching the higher latitudes of Ft. Davis, we drove through the town of Pecos, in relatively flat terrain, irrigated. Sweet cantaloupes and tomatoes are among the chief products. The smell of tomatoes in the field—not the plants themselves but some chemical sprayed on them—was so penetrating that to this day I react nostalgically to it (a bit like Proust) and choose West Texas tomatoes at the supermarket having the same aroma, evoking those distant orbs, poppy-red in their green cradles,

Alpine was reached by Texas 118, from the north. In town it met US 90, the standard route west from Houston and San Antonio. At that point 90 is coextensive with US 67 from the northeast (Ft. Stockton). The road heads west to Marfa; then 67 turns south to the Mexican border. None of these roads carried heavy traffic. Today, cross-country drivers ordinarily take I-10 and no longer see any of this. Many travelers hated the area. But for those who can see well, the whole region has great beauties. Nothing like those of Switzerland, despite the name *Alpine*; its own.

My father rested in the daytime. Sometimes he took me in the afternoon to get a Coke at City Drugs, which, unlike its rival, Alpine Rexall Drugstore, had a fountain and counter. His sole work that winter was taking the federal census, a job he carried out conscientiously. Budgets were strict. At first we lived in a one-room cottage in a compound built for GI couples at the local college, Sul Ross State. I call Sul Ross a "cow college"; the most popular majors were education and range animal husbandry. It was then and remains the smallest of the Texas State University System. My mother was able to get a job as a grader in English; her two degrees and experience were worth something.

The cottage was a bit tight for a couple with an adolescent daughter. Thus, after some time we moved to a three-room garage apartment, adequate, if not roomy. My bed was in the living room. No desk, as I remember. Where did I do my homework? At the kitchen table, I suppose. I was enrolled in the high school, of course, as a junior, though I was only fifteen years of age, because of extra credits I had in solid subjects, which enabled me to graduate from high school at seventeen. Socially, I fitted in well enough.

I owe my Rice education to geographical and meteorological factors. Even with high temperatures, dry West Texas summers are much more tolerable than steamy ones. In Houston then, air conditioning was unusual. The Rice classrooms, offices, and apartments for young faculty and out-of-town women students, in one of which I would live for four years, had none. Two Rice professors of English spent summers at Sul Ross, giving the modest place a bit of cachet, making a little money, and avoiding Gulf Coast humidity. One visitor was Wilfred S. Dowden, a specialist on Romanticism, destined to shine as an authority on Thomas Moore. In the summer of 1950, my mother was assigned to grade for him. There were social exchanges with him and his wife at which I was present. He invited me to look into Rice. Why not? You make your own luck if it isn't there; you use it if it is.

That same summer, having, apparently, decided to remain in Alpine, my parents purchased, with funds that must have been in a Denver bank, a modest four-room house. Photographs taken there touch me: my father on the front steps, wearing a western shirt and broad-brimmed hat, like most western men; two other high school girls and I; pictures from a party, when we were dressed up; many years later, my mother, holding Kate.

The front yard was surrounded by a low white fence, of the Kentucky Blue Grass style, but without that same soft grass; only sturdier varieties could survive. The back consisted of two areas. The smaller had the same tough grass and a picnic table, where we ate many meals. The larger was left in the state of nature; water was too expensive and labor too great (in Father's view) to keep it in grass. Would that others, there and especially in the great water-guzzling cities of the Southwest (I have in mind Phoenix, Las Vegas, and Los Angeles) would follow his good example. In time, he ordered seedlings from catalogues; dutifully watered by hand but without waste, they became trees and eventually contributed stateliness to what was otherwise a plain property.

In fall 1950, my father was hired at the high school as an English teacher. In the meantime, Mother had found a job in Marathon, thirty-one miles via highway 90 to the east, to which she car-pooled. Not a plum job. She did so in the knowledge that, wherever I went to college the following year, money would be needed. Father and I went home together for lunch, called by many "dinner." Mother told me I must prepare him a hot meal. With no interest in cooking, I nevertheless learned enough for the purpose.

That my father was outstanding in his classroom was attested by numerous students and by Mrs. Blucher, the other high school English teacher and his supervisor. He was popular; quality is recognized usually by even ordinary minds. The best testimony to his skills was offered by Hobson Wildenthal, a student of his, the son of the Sul Ross president, newly arrived at the college. Dr. Wildenthal must have been displeased by what he found among the faculty. The level of preparation was embarrassingly low, partly because many had doctorates in education only; they and numerous others possessed very little experience of the world of learning. (One professor in the humanities expressed surprise upon learning that Ireland was an island.) Hobson, knowing that his father wished to raise the level of teaching skills and intellect, told him about Mr. Hill, saying he would be a fine addition to the faculty. President Wildenthal listened. My father was hired for the following school year and remained there, with interruptions, until 1969, the year of his death.

The hiring was on the condition that he obtain a master's degree of some sort; Dr. Wildenthal was attentive to the faculty profile. It could be done at Sul Ross. With his sense of husbandry, or economy (an aspect of prudence), and with permission from the dean of the Graduate School, a Dr. Casey, himself an English professor, who became his thesis director, Father devised a way to use material already written: he would create a critical context for his short stories set in the American west. He had written them in Denver and, under the name "Victor Hill," had tried to peddle them for extra income. No takers. They were, I believe, too refined, too nuanced. But they could furnish the central portion of a thesis dealing with the popular genre of the Western. In short, he presented creative work in a critical framework. From time to time I reread his fiction, always with profit.

What Father gave to those who sought out his courses and counsel was invaluable. During lengthy office hours, mandated by the state, he helped students, sometimes line by line, write better and understand more. He offered encouragement and suggested, to the better ones, goals. His view was that despite the curricular limitations at Sul Ross and its utterly parochial character, one could get there, by judicious choice of electives and major, a reasonably good education and a foundation for future work in several fields. Hobson himself illustrated the point; though as an undergraduate at his father's institution he had not majored in physics—maybe there was no such major—he got a Ph.D. in the field elsewhere and was an eminent researcher until he moved into administrative positions.

My father was also a superb teacher at home. Like other good parents, of course, he taught mostly by example. Neither actions nor words were lost on me; they were golden. He would offer an observation, cite a guideline, and give good reasons why one should follow it. He noted more than once that I should avoid saying things that would hurt others. "Remember what the great Lord Nelson said" was a familiar phrase ("England expects every man to do his duty"). It was perhaps directed to himself as much as me. Lessons in severe tones about serious matters were rare; anger even rarer (twice, perhaps). Like him, I do not indulge in anger. Since 1987, I have not lost my temper. Irritation, yes, sometimes, but controlled, usually concealed. Furor, no. Memories of a close friend losing her temper and shouting at me, in public, are painful.

A part of my father's good example and oral teaching was his excellent judgment. He knew a fool when he encountered him but— the classroom excepted—rarely lost time trying to correct anyone. He understood the dangers or foolishness of aggrandizement. Why, he asked, was bigger always better? Well, if money is involved, yes, one thinks. Not necessarily; even for others; surely not for him, as his choices demonstrate. Health and happiness may suffer from the "More money, more" syndrome. Look at the swollen population of this nation, the deteriorated environment, polluted waters, enormous dunes of foul, undegradable trash, depleted water tables and aquifers, city living conditions for some that rival Blake's visions of dark satanic mills.

In addition to guiding me by precept and example, and seeing to various wants, what did Father do for the household? He took care of the mail and finances, going to the post office in Alpine (no house delivery for many years) and writing checks. He was the gardener, in charge of setting and resetting the watering hose. He assisted often with grocery shopping, unpacking the sacks, sorting, and searching for any roaches or other bugs they might introduce. He also helped in the kitchen by drying dishes.

He quoted well-known phrases and lines from both poetry and prose. "O tempora! O mores!" and "Jacta alea est"—underlining his concern with fate. Of course he knew his Shakespeare, whom he held in high honor.

> There is a tide in the affairs of men
>
> which, taken at the flood, leads on to fortune;
>
> omitted, all the voyage of their lives
>
> is bound in shallows and in miseries.[6]

He was fond of the pastoral genre in general and Gray's most famous elegy. Perhaps gazing out at the nearly barren landscape around us, he would roll off with pleasure these famous lines: "Full many a flower is born to blush unseen / And waste its sweetness on the desert air." *Et in arcadia ego.* Robert Burns would make an appearance:

> Wee, sleekit, cow'rin, tim'rous beastie,
>
> O, what panic's in thy breastie.

He liked Chaucer also; Milton, somewhat less. Still, I heard frequently the latter's immortal line from the sonnet on his blindness: "They also serve who only stand and wait." Surely. But that is not an invitation to idleness.

Modern Irish drama caught my father's interest, though he found it as a rule wrenching. Appreciating perhaps the poet's irony, he accepted the early T. S. Eliot, especially "The Love Song of J. Alfred

---

[6] *Julius Caesar*, IV, iii.

Paul Hill in England

Prufrock": "I grow old, I grow old, / I shall wear my trousers rolled." His repeated quoting of the opening lines of Yeats's "The Lake Isle of Innisfree"—in gentle mockery, not admiration—is so etched in me that it led me recently before quite a learned assembly to confess, with apologies, that I did not like Yeats much. I should have said that I *could* not. Of course I acknowledge outstanding Yeats poems such as "Among School Children" and "Sailing to Byzantium." Moreover, I am not insensitive to him as a figure of the artist. I quoted him in my poem "Yeats and Maud Gonne, 1891": "To be a poet, first you have to be / a man."[23]

Father routinely offered little witticisms and made jokes. Laugh so that you may not weep—very Irish. In private, he would play with the names of those for whom he had little respect. Professor Bridgewater easily became "Professor Bilgewater," and Dr. Blackwell, "Dr. Quackwell." A woman's girth might draw a crack: "We must make sure that she has enough to eat at our party." He remarked often on the beauty of the rangeland or mountain vistas, genuinely touched, and was courtesy personified to everyone. In short, he looked on the world with implied or overt benevolence. Indeed, he was an idealist, a dreamer, not a doer. He liked James Thurber's Walter Mitty and often alluded to him, something of an alter ego, as he recognized. In that respect—the dreamer—he resembled, I think, his brother Jack.

In the late 1950s, my parents took a ship to Alaska. Next, they crossed the Atlantic, sailing from Montreal, to spend a summer in the British Isles. Father was enchanted with the beauty, cultural heritage, and quaint ways of his ancestors' lands. He wanted to go back and stay longer. He was willing to spend for that purpose sums he would not have parted with otherwise. The will was there; it identified the opportunity. That's what serendipity is, often. Not one to pull strings—neither insinuating himself slyly nor glad-handing—he could act, very effectively. He investigated possibilities for Anglophone foreigners to teach in England and got himself hired as a Fellow of Balliol College of Oxford for 1962-1963. He would handle American literature classes in its extension program at satellite locations. Sul Ross granted him a leave of absence. He and Mother were received graciously everywhere. The English year lasted, for him, fifteen months; Mother returned stateside somewhat sooner. The winter of that year was exceedingly cold. Father did not like the cold, as you will remember. Yet they lived for a while in a leased flat heated by a meager stove for which he had to carry sacks of coal up a steep hill. For him, the game was worth the candle. We know that everything has its price; pay it or do without.

Thus, in summer 1962, crossing by ferry from France, where I was doing research in the Bibliothèque Nationale, I met my parents in Kent. My visit was short but delightful. We traveled around, staying at old inns, including the Flying Horse in Boughton Aluph, near Ashford. Then we crossed the Channel from Folkstone to Amsterdam, my mother wishing to see the most famous city of the Netherlands, its picturesque architecture, and its canals. Paris was next. I remember strolling with them along the Champs-Elysées and having lunch somewhere there, maybe the Georges V, where Vivaldi's *Seasons* was the choice for background music.

Upon returning to Alpine more than a year later, Father took up his post at Sul Ross. But he was restless. By spring 1969, he had announced his retirement. He had made a little money from investments—Aunt Flora gave him tips sometimes—and the family savings were adequate for his new plan, which was to move to England permanently. Mother found that excessive. The Lower Rio Grande Valley one year; Alpine; England for one year ... She had agreed. But to put an ocean permanently between herself, her habits, and her sisters, her friends was too much. Her rejection was firm. She is not to be blamed; it was a radical plan, at their age, an uprooting she viewed as irreparable.

I believe Father put no pressure on Mother, beyond the plan itself, to indulge him. He could only accept her decree, following the counsel of Descartes I quoted earlier, to act on oneself. One must give in to others. But we are all others. To others; we press them simply by existing. It is now thought, erroneously maybe, that doing violence to one's deepest self may be harmful. He retired definitively from Sul Ross—mentally he had already separated himself, I think—and found part time work as a clerk at a modest motel (there was no other kind in those parts). But, not truly resigned to staying, he started planning a compromise measure, whereby he and Mother would move back to Colorado, neither Denver nor Colorado Springs but north, in the Loveland area or farther, toward Wyoming. Where was his dread of the cold? It was overridden, I think, by his dislike of cities (except London) and by his restless angst, which no doctoring, no medicine, could have relieved. (That he eschewed "physic" and did not frequent doctors or believe in them should not be viewed as shedding unfavorable light on family members who pursued the profession; he honored them but—perhaps for that very reason—stayed away from others.) How far the new plans would have gone I do not know: he died in early November that same year.

There was no prior indication of heart failure; but he had not had cardiac tests. Could his clogged organ have been discovered? He had smoked for some years, even during my childhood. The salt pills he took to offset the West Texas heat may have left damage; and he did not exercise. In bed one night, around two AM, he turned over repeatedly. Mother, wakened, made some remark. He said, "I'm restless." After a few moments, she turned on a light; she found his face all purple. She phoned her doctor. When he came, it was, of course, too late; Father was gone, probably, by the time she looked at him.

Why have I been granted these long years while he had comparatively few? It was fate, the fate of the body and what the essayist Joseph Epstein labels "the contingency of events." Does this fate have agency? Verdi wrote of "the Force of Destiny." Do we feel it? One summer, my parents spent time in the high Colorado mountains near Winter Park, where Jean and Dwight ran a lodge, popular with skiers in snow season and summer visitors from the Plains states. Dwight owned an old school bus in which he drove sightseers around the territory, notably up Rollins Pass, which crosses the Continental Divide. It is a former railroad bed, used before the Moffat Tunnel was constructed, subsequently redesigned as a road. My father joined a tour. The bus arrived at a narrow old trestle. Dwight invited his passengers to get out and walk across if they wished. My father alone remained. He had confidence in Dwight, of course. He also knew that his string had not yet run out.

Fate, we know, is a joker; she loves twists, irony, pratfalls. He would have appreciated (intellectually) the ironic trajectory of an American poet named Henry Lee, Lt. US Army. He was part of the Bataan Death March and until early 1945 was in the Catapatuan prison camp. Having survived in those hellish conditions, though terribly undernourished and weakened, he was removed by the Japanese and put in the hold of a ship to be sent to the home islands as a slave laborer. He died en route to Japan with 1,600 others when the ship was bombed by American planes.[7]

---

7   His poems were discovered concealed under a shack in the camp. They were published in the *Saturday Evening Post* in December 1945. The following poem, untitled, must reflect his misery and suffering there. His personal philosophy is evident.
I could not know the meaning nor the way
I was not one with all that time must end
Until one hopeless, joyous, bitter day
I looked on unmasked death and saw a friend

Flora Hill

Chapter Six

A Portrait of Aunt Flora

Flora Kathleen Hill, born in January 1900, deserves a prominent place in these memoirs. Starting in my childhood, her presence in my life was enormous. She was also part of my middle adulthood, when both my parents as well as my grandparents were gone.

Seven years separated her from my father; nonetheless they were very close. As a girl, she had rheumatic fever; under Grandfather's orders, she had to stay in bed. I have a small English bone china chocolate cup and saucer that were hers, perhaps from those years. She, bedridden, and my father, too young to go out with the others, became dependent children together. He may have grasped better than they what deprivation meant to her. For circumstantial reasons or genetic ones, they were much alike. Jack, between them in age, resembled them both.

Since, during my father's first years, she called him "Baby," he retaliated by using the same name. Turned into "Babe"; it became a name of brotherly affection and remained in his vocabulary ever after, appearing in conversation and correspondence. A silly side, less characteristic of Mary and Kenneth, came out often in the pair, as I observed them. I am much like her, notably in our rather androgynous mental makeup (not physical).

Flora Hill and Paul Hill Going Fishing, Colorado

Poems of mine reflect what I imagine of her illness and the isolation—that is, what they did to her, or for her, as I understand it. Bed rest was the only cure (not always successful); but children do not want to rest, unless they are very ill, as in fact sometimes she was. Her confinement was hard on everyone in the household, Grandmother and Aunt Mary particularly. Grandmother was her chief teacher; Mary, the older girl, was obliged to assist Grandmother and to give up some of her pleasures. (I'll return to that topic.)[1]

After seven years as an invalid, Aunt Flora did get well enough to mature and lead a full life, though one lung remained bad and she was not much more than five feet in height. Grandmother, who was Mary's first keyboard instructor, must have given Aunt Flora lessons. She chose the organ over the piano, perhaps in order to assert her distinction from her sister, who had the advantages of age and health. Bach occupied the first place in Flora's pantheon. In the familiar mode, she favored Scottish ballads, some centuries-old. She was tutored, then went to a private preparatory school and the University of Denver.

I do not know at what age she was given an IQ test. Her score was very high. Her field of study was chemistry. I have mentioned her MS degree from the University of Michigan. Until age seventy, she was employed, whether by Hill & Hill Laboratories, others' medical practices, or hospitals. In the 1940s she worked at Children's Hospital. She nearly always missed the family dinners at Thanksgiving and Christmas; though deserving holidays off, according to the rotation arrangement, she would get calls saying she was needed because others were sick or had "a family emergency."

Having been ill so long, she appreciated life enormously and was a very positive person. Few shadows appeared on her face, with its sparkling eyes; her voice was touched only infrequently with a tone of unpleasantness. She loved play and games of many sorts. With Mary, Kenneth, and others, she played bridge. She was generous. She liked to bestow impromptu gifts. She did so for me once at a

---

[1] See the poems "The Sparrow," "Gloves," "Heart," and "Old Fashioneds" in previous collections and "Kirs," forthcoming.

shop on Dublin Street during a visit to New Orleans, choosing, after trying out my taste for various objects, a small enameled pot from the Indian subcontinent. It is displayed on my piano with other Asian objects. When Kate and I crossed the Atlantic with the aunts on the *Queen Elizabeth II* in 1981, Flora, charmed by the shops, not only spent time selecting gifts to take back to Denver but also bought things for Kate and me; my gift was a narrow silk scarf, cream-colored, with the Christian Dior logo in blue.

Her imagination was active and vivid. Surely she had exercised it during those years in bed; wouldn't you? She anticipated our travels with enormous pleasure and recalled them similarly. With exceptions, my poems enchanted her by their poetic and visual images. (Some in *Watering*, she said, were "so sad!") Like the rest of the family, she relished being in the mountains. She liked *Gemütlichkeit* in restaurants and houses and had an eye for attractive domestic architecture. As we drove around regions of France, she would spy an appealing house (no larger than a manor house—a chateau would not have suited us) or small rustic dwelling on a slope and, picturing already our retreat or holiday there, say, "Let's buy that one!"

She was astute in reading character. Perhaps it was a natural gift; perhaps it came from reading in bed as a child (on her good days) and Grandmother's guidance. She knew fools when she saw them— too often—and disliked strongly all selfishness, oafishness, cruelty. She told me that she could not forgive the strikers in Seattle who had viciously beaten Uncle Jack. "God will have to forgive them." Though, like my father, showing generally the very spirit of courtesy, she was not above anger. When her Gaelic temper was set off, woe to those who were its target! She particularly disliked large people who, with or without intention, pushed others around (she was an easy target, physically). Again, like him, she valued experience, a special kind of knowledge, and she was willing to pay for it.

Her appreciation of the visible (mountains, cathedral, quaint village, colorful garden, elegant bridge) was keen. Moreover, she retained as an adult certain extrasensory abilities that are seen occasionally in young girls but normally disappear before age

Flora Hill and Catharine, Summer 1985

twenty. The gift was attested clearly at least once. Mary was in Montreal, or so it was thought. Flora, sitting with Grandmother on the front porch, said, as a streetcar came up the East Alameda hill, "Mary is on that streetcar." Indeed she was; taking advantage of changed circumstances, she had left Québec sooner than expected and, reaching Denver and the Union Station, calmly took streetcar 8 home. No need for the drama of a telephone call or telegram.

Another eerie incident is the following, which took place immediately after Flora's death. Jack Miller, Jean's younger son, had been invited to live with the aunts pending his wedding, when he would move to a small house he and his bride, Jeannie, had purchased in west Denver. He slept in the basement, in an open area near the staircase leading to the front hallway. He and Aunt Flora were close. Before going to a hospital (and dying after a week or so), she said to him, "I shall come back and haunt you." Jesting? Both liked jokes, but I think rather that she felt some tie with the house that would not be loosened easily. One night Jack heard the characteristic creak of the front door, a heavy oaken door, well locked at night. Some while later, the sound was repeated. In the morning, the door was properly locked and bore no sign of any forced entry.

Aunt Flora understood and tolerated the body much better than my mother. She could even make a joke referring to bodies, women's and men's; such would not have entered my mother's mind. Occasional comments of Flora's were intended for a very small audience only—consisting of Jean's husband, Dwight, or me, perhaps. She was an omnivorous reader and strove constantly to learn, partly by studying people, also by being curious and looking up things that might interest her. In the second of my grandparents' houses, which had a sunny breakfast nook, a bookcase held a multivolume encyclopedia of small format. She had acquired it gratis by shopping regularly at some grocery store. A volume or so would come out for consultation in the course of an informal lunch.

Like the dining table and parlor, that little nook was the scene of long conversations. To be sure, in proper families, as readers are doubtless aware, one did not talk about money, politics, religion, or sex; there was general agreement anyway, and nothing more need be said. (Readers may observe also that those four topics are not addressed here often either.) Nor was much time spent on household trivia (something needing repair, or recipes, all boring to me in my girlhood and remaining so). But conversation still ranged very widely.

Following the example of her British-Canadian mother, Aunt Flora drank strong tea. In her later working years, she began the morning with coffee but, as I remember it, after her morning cup had tea also. Grandfather likewise took coffee, needing, in his old age, its stronger stimulation. He made his own, boiled in a saucepan and strained. As for Aunt Mary, "tea and toast" was her formula for almost any indisposition.

Did my mother play second fiddle to Aunt Flora in my affections and know it? Probably, and I regret it. Like grandparents, an aunt has an easy role. The responsibilities of rearing the child fall on those in the inner circle; even coming from the extended family, the outsiders have what the French call *le beau rôle*. Aunt Flora could be silly, as I noted, a wonderful advantage in dealing with a child. She was also more reflective, thus making observations, now practical, now philosophical, that would not occur to Mother. She was the image of diplomacy in her dealings with others—save on the occasions I have alluded to, when she lost her temper and spoke spitefully. I was never the target of such ire.

Flora's relationship with her elder sister can bear examination. Far from smooth, it was, fundamentally, unhappy. I regret it; I loved them both. (Aunt Mary also has her poems, connected to her piano playing and experiences.) But rivalry was built into the family situation, as it is into human nature. Mary and Grandmother were very close in some ways, sharing a bank account, for instance. Mary had the disadvantage, however, to be well, while Flora was ill and in need of daily attention, dependent on others for survival-level care. Mary's childhood was interrupted also, thus. In their adulthood, they were often apart. Until she was obliged to retire at age seventy, Mary taught in various Colorado towns. Each sister may have felt that it was a good arrangement. When both parents were gone, they finally lived with each other. I could still sense tension sometimes. Not long before dying, Aunt Flora told me, as a sort of testimony, that her sister had been "mean" to her.

My father's feelings were shaped for a lifetime by the situation. When we arrived from Texas at the family house, he would greet his elder sister with the simple phrase "Hello, Mary"; it lacked warmth. He did not correspond with her. She was an unwilling and dilatory correspondent anyhow. Was that due to the conviction that others did not care much about her? (Yet in fact I am not the only one who loved her and took pleasure in her company.)

To compensate for her small stature, one supposes, Aunt Flora liked big and powerful automobiles: a dark green Packard, a "Fluid Drive" De Soto. When, in her last years, she wanted a new car, she went shopping at a Buick dealership. A short-sighted salesman, seeing the "little lady" in what must have been very unimposing attire, without makeup or jewelry, suggested that she would not be able to afford a model she admired. She had *in cash* in her purse the necessary bills. Angels come upon us unawares, don't they? She went next door to the Dodge dealer and chose a fine claret-red model.

In those big land cruisers, she drove fast. Going down one of the Front Range passes on a Sunday afternoon in summer toward Denver, with hundreds of others who had been at higher elevations for the day or weekend, she would pass, in her impatience, long lines of cars ahead of her. Vroom! Fate protected her against meeting one, just one, nudging out from the opposite direction and coming with similar speed. Such an encounter would have meant instant death.

She was devoted to all the nieces and nephews, with whom she corresponded and whom she welcomed for visits. For years, she and I spoke by telephone nearly every Saturday morning. She had many friends, including correspondents in Modesto, California, where she had once worked, and numerous Denver women who were patients of the doctor in whose offices she was a lab technician in her last years of employment. They would get to know her, then invite her to lunch; then she would invite them. One or two gave her expensive gifts. She saw couples socially also, and she had Japanese-American friends, not wishing to turn away those not connected to the bloodshed during the war.

The table settings at her luncheons were beautiful (I remember a lavender linen tablecloth and exquisite china), and she served gourmet dishes, quite complicated compared to the cuisine Grandmother had offered. (You know, however, that I still honor it and often want it.) I fancied particularly Aunt Flora's mini-meat loaves, prepared in muffin tins. I never managed to make any so tasty as hers.

The aunts, Kate, and I traveled together on five occasions, beginning with our transatlantic voyage, to which I alluded above, and travels in France and England. I must mention a fellow passenger on that crossing, "The Man from Yonkers," who paid court to Flora and expressed interest in marriage. Yonkers! And she was eighty-one! She did not encourage him. Flora and Kate established a strong bond of companionship on that journey. (Her way with children was extraordinary, since, I suppose, she was one at heart.)

In France we had a rental car, in which we drove from Cherbourg to Dijon. She sat with Kate in the back while Aunt Mary and I occupied the front seat. Flora was an enthusiastic visitor, liking almost everything, smiling, exchanging greetings in hotels and restaurants. She liked men, and they liked her; witness the waiters—and the great writer Jules Roy, knowledgeable about feminine worth, who fell, or wanted to fall, in love with her. That was obvious, despite the language barrier: though he had flown RAF planes from British bases during World War II, he had not kept up what English he had learned, and she no longer had much command of French. But you don't have to exchange words to love: an eminent reviewer in Louisiana said, after having read the essay "Aunt Flora in My Retroscope," that he was in love with her, that is, the woman she had been.

Subsequently, we took other journeys together: in 1982, a long road trip, through Colorado, Wyoming (the Tetons and Yellowstone), then back to Colorado and on to New Mexico; in 1983, San Francisco by train, then Alaska, by cruise ship; Louisiana and Mississippi at Christmastime by car that same year, to visit plantation houses;

finally, the Caribbean. In Biloxi, Mississippi, at an historic hotel since razed to create something more attractive to gamblers, I remember how each aunt expressed to me her appreciation for driving them around; and how in the dining room people at adjacent tables admired us, the three-generation foursome. These travels enabled Kate to know her grandparents' generation, despite having then no grandparents. We last traveled together in summer 1985. After they flew to New Orleans, I drove us all to Ft. Lauderdale, where we embarked on a cruise through the islands. These elderly women were a joy. As on previous cruises, we did well at Team Trivia, with our three generations' worth of knowledge. Flora wanted to go to France the next summer, to visit the coast around Biarritz. It could not be.

Why Flora did not marry has never been elucidated to my satisfaction. Perhaps because Mary, the elder, had not? At one time, the latter may have been interested in a man in Montreal; she never spoke of him in my presence, and the story is clouded in time. As a rule Mary did not have friends, neither men nor women; or I recall none. She spoke of the woman with whom she boarded during her years teaching in Holyoke, Colorado, as "Mrs. Clarkson."

In contrast, Flora once mentioned an Irishman who had made her little heart "go pitty-pat." Where might that have been? At the University of Michigan? In Modesto? Once, for reasons I no longer recall, I needed to borrow from her a nightgown. She opened a drawer, looked among its contents, and pulled out a beautiful white garment, made of lawn or other light goods, with embroidery across the top. "You'll look like a queen in this one," she said. What dreams might she have had, not only in her youth? I think she had not known the woman's joy of presenting herself to a loving, desiring man. But surely she could imagine it.

Like her mother, Aunt Flora was both strong and weak. Colds, to which she was prone, would last sometimes for weeks. She was small-boned as well as short of stature, but muscular, with good biceps; and she had endurance. When she was older, she suffered stoically through the dreaded winter months, their cold, their gloom. Her hands bothered her; she could not stand gloves and thus had chapped fingers for long weeks. Why didn't I—living in the Sunbelt—do more to ease the winters by inviting the aunts at least once a season down south? But my domestic situation was not always calm; visitors would have added friction. So I chose, alas, the easier course.

Since Mary was away for the school year, Flora was the chief caretaker of her old parents; it was her turn then. She helped Grandmother through her illnesses and dying; she took care of Grandfather, returning home from her work downtown at lunchtime during his last years to see to his needs. Sometime after his death, the aunts moved to an entirely residential neighborhood farther east in Denver. The move was inspired by Aunt Flora's dislike of traffic sounds, which had increased along Josephine Street.

The house, on Jersey Street, had a large back garden, in which a handsome birch tree stood sentinel. Workmen tended the lawn, but it was Flora who chose the shrubbery and cultivated seasonal flowers, liking roses especially. That was the house at which Paul Brosman and I celebrated our wedding at the Denver courthouse in August 1970 by a family lunch and to which we traveled by car in summer 1972 to introduce Kate to the family. We had with us also our cat, Spookie, who, given the fine furnishings in the house, was confined to quarters in the garage. He was not much the worse for it: he received visitors often and otherwise amused himself by pawing and leaping at moths.

When Uncle Kenneth, whom the aunts saw frequently, died the next year, they decided to purchase his house from his estate; the heirs all lived elsewhere. A raised patio attached to the house was transformed into a warm-weather dining room, with windows on two sides. That's where Aunt Flora liked to have luncheons and where afternoon tea and many meals were served. She would bring out a cake at teatime or after dinner, announcing, "I baked it with my own little hands." She beamed, knowing full well that we had seen in the kitchen a box labeled "Volmer's Bakery." The house had been the house of death but became again one of happiness; Jean's children spent weeks there and visitors came and went. After my mother died, I traveled there for a short post-Christmas stay. Those few days, which included the anniversary of Grandmother's death, helped the aunts and me alike, as I ached for family company.

At Christmastime of 1985, suffering a recurrence of the cancer she had beaten earlier, Aunt Flora was too weak to purchase presents for others, even by phone or mail. She died in February. I flew up for her memorial service, held in the Cathedral of St. John the Divine. One of the great-nephews was at the organ, and all the nephews and nieces of my generation were present, as well as Aunt Mary. According to her wishes, Aunt Flora was cremated, like Grandfather. Jean arranged for household help for Mary, who spent a week with John in Illinois that summer. She lingered until late October. "The oldest hath borne most; we that are young / will never see so much, nor live so long." Later, another great-nephew, James Miller, hiked up Mount Sneffles in the San Juans to scatter her ashes.[2]

---

[2] *King Lear,* v, iii.

Part II

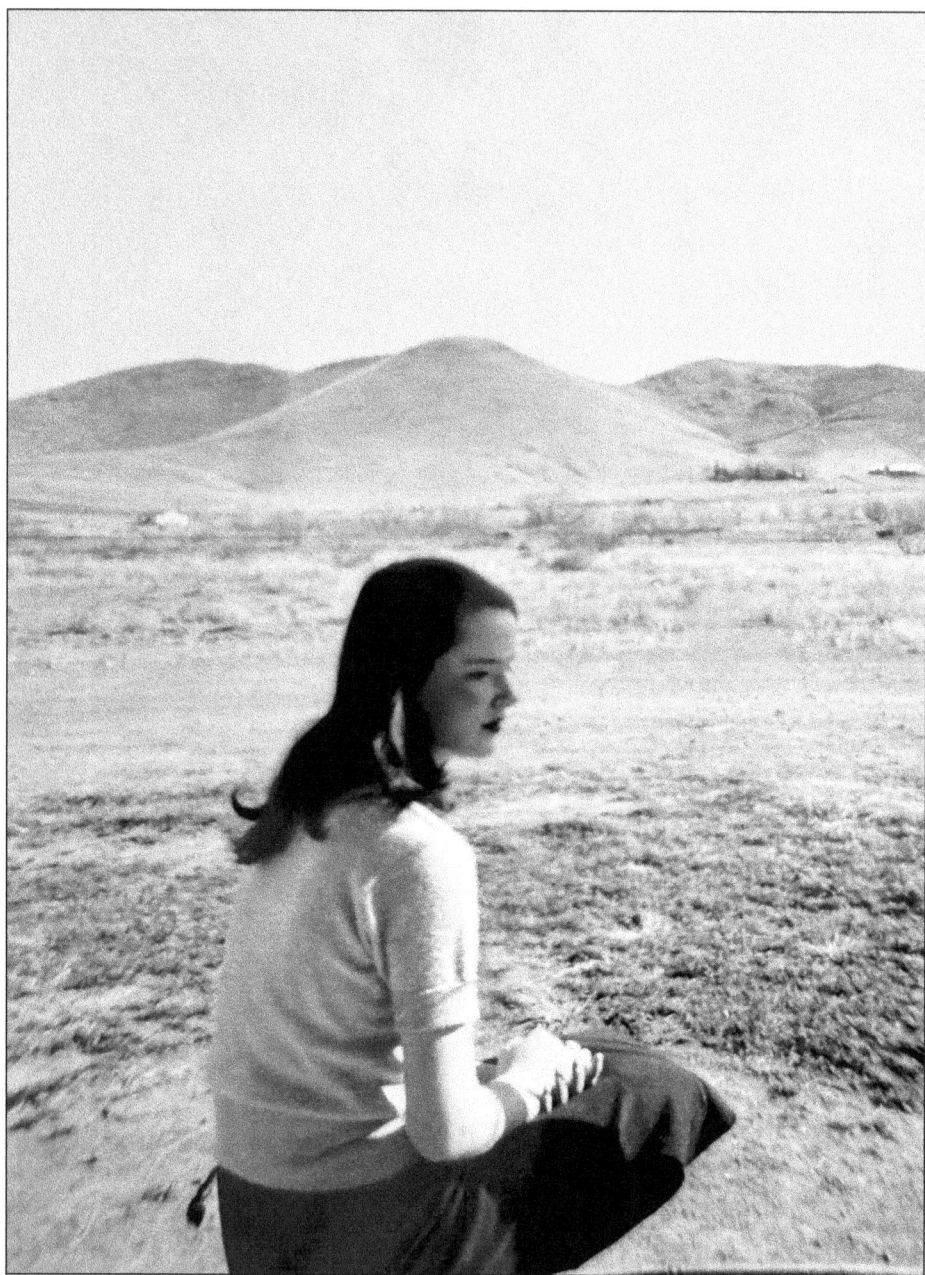

Catharine Seated, Alpine, circa *1950*

Chapter Seven

The Girl, the Woman

The girl visible in previous chapters evoking my parents and their families and my years in their company became the woman glimpsed already occasionally and depicted in the remainder of these memoirs. Some cataloguing of traits and actions, beginning in adolescence, is necessary here.

I shall deal first with my positions regarding certain social expectations, some connected to my sex. I resisted them because of my strong sense of my own being, that is, autonomy. When I was a schoolgirl—seven or eight, perhaps—as John Hall knocked at the back screen door one morning asking for me, I appeared and spoke to him in my pajamas. "You must not let John see you in your pajamas," said Mother afterwards. Why not? Oh, mercy. Is it what "the neighbors might think"? But why care? Apart from my elders in the family and a few teachers, I cared little, as I have written, for others' judgments. Or was it the adult's reaction, anticipatory and premature, to what the young man John would become later might think, reflecting on the neighbor girl in unsuitable garb?

Nevertheless, like Gide, I was in some ways an inhibited child and long remained so. And like his mother, I cannot easily breach convention, at least without good reason. Never would I attempt to invade a masculine space—men's club, athletic facility, and so on. Nor would I go where I was not wanted for other reasons. During my last visit to Vienna, in the 1990s, an Austrian acquaintance (not an intimate friend), an architect, without manners, despite his distinction in other ways, obliged me to enter a large hotel reception room where medical conventioneers had gathered. He knew he was crashing the party. I objected in a low voice, but he was pleased with himself, pleased to show me off and entertain me at no expense. I recalled two similar episodes during an earlier visit, one at a fancy wine-tasting, one at a Vespers service. For neither was I prepared; he had not advised me ahead of time to change my blazer and flat shoes for more suitable attire. He pushed me onto people at the wine party, then to the front pew as the service was in progress.

Well, Vienna was his city; New Orleans is mine. When, during a subsequent visit there, he bragged about doing the same thing at a private party at the Pontchartrain Hotel on an evening when I had to leave him to his own devices, I was disgusted. And when, much worse, he insulted, by saying what no one should say, two young women working the entry line for a riverboat cruise, I was outraged; he ceased that day to be my friend.[1]

Yet inhibitions and a strong sense of the conventional are not the entire picture. There is boldness in me also, as there was in Gide. (He violated glaringly various prohibitions and, much more than I, did foolish, nay, dangerous things.) If it is proper for me to enter, say, a small library frequented by so few that its regulars treat it like a club or sanctuary and rather resent intrusions, I enter anyhow. When I was not yet seventeen, I was with other Alpine High students in a school bus en route across Texas for a scholastic meeting. One of the girls realized that she was in need of a feminine sanitary product. The bus stopped somewhere, maybe Abilene. A drugstore was visible. But she whispered that she dared not go buy what she needed; she would be too embarrassed. (I suppose her mother bought those products for her.) Other girls seated near us kept mute. I volunteered to go for her.

---

[1] See "Sazeracs," in *Aerosols and Other Poems*. "On the Danube," in *An Aesthetic Education and Other Stories*, uses certain details of a visit I paid to him in Vienna and depicts the chief character favorably, but the plot is of my invention.

Paul Hill and Catharine Hill, in Alpine, 1955

In fact, I am intimidated by no one, high or low. Indeed, if the late queen of Great Britain or the current monarch invited me to luncheon, I should prepare myself by studying the appropriate etiquette but would not in the least be awed. Once my friend Evelyn asked me not to invite to a party at which she would be present a professor at whose feet we had both studied. "She intimidates me," she had to confess. Yet it was not because of any indifferent performance in class; she was an excellent student. No; it was something else. Without experiencing it myself, I recognized how that could be, as she had recognized in me something she did not have but could appreciate and thus even live, so to speak, vicariously.[2]

How can I be both bold in some ways and sensitive to social expectations concerning appearance and behavior? Ah, it depends in what context, and for whom. My parents strove to teach me that the outward person (dress, manners) does count; and they succeeded in doing so by means of patience and, eventually, the help of pressures from elsewhere. Proper attire, comportment, and speech are social badges and even armor; like credentials, they allow one to pass in and out of gatherings and associations without ado. One can then even venture to make a pointed comment or correct others. I recall a Christmas party in my building, for which a written invitation was sent out with "suggested attire." A fellow comes dressed in a nondescript short-sleeved shirt, khaki cargo shorts, and heavy hiking boots and thick socks. Those are not credentials for the occasion. Unlike me in Vienna, he was told what to wear. He was putting himself above others, following his own code. But that is offensive; who is he to decide the norms for the event? In fact, he was thus putting himself below others.

More generally speaking, what do superficial sartorial restrictions have to do with personal value and achievement? (That is the schoolgirl reasoning. There's something of the schoolgirl left in me.) Why did they even exist in the twentieth century, since women—including my mother and three aunts—were already widely present in the work force and often needed very practical, sometimes protec-

---

[2] See the poem "Evelyn," in *On the North Slope*.

tive clothing? Looking at the details of the matter, I note that skirts ceased falling to the floor after the Great War, which, like its sequel, altered women's lives radically: the custom of covering a woman from shoulders to toes in a sort of tent had lost its dominion. "Bathing costumes" had similarly shrunken, becoming in my girlhood brief affairs covering only the torso. We had zippers, to which we now add Velcro; their superiority over buttons is obvious. Practicality, even ease; that's what we need.

In this connection I note that my mother, while remaining attached to various uses of her girlhood, gave up others, including the long skirts I alluded to. Fortunately. But she did not adopt trousers of any sort except jodhpurs, on rare occasions; a photograph, taken on a hiking expedition during my parents' courtship or early marriage, shows her thus clad. No slacks of any sort appeared in her wardrobe later—a pity, I thought, because they, along with a looser hairdo (she wore tight curls) and less beige in her wardrobe, would have helped her look younger. I suppose many of us are reluctant to change: "Be not the first by whom the new is tried, / Nor yet the last to lay the old aside." But Alexander Pope himself surely realized that his maxim could not apply universally. While counseling us to avoid extremes, he must have understood that innovation was desirable (think of navigation) and that we can all profit from *some* novelty. Even extremes have their place. Great geniuses have to be extreme in their fields; Leonardo was extreme in more than one.

Presently, I favor a quasi-universal style, with trousers (not too tight, please, for women), shirt or blouse, and jacket, if suitable. Skirts merely call attention to the lower anatomy of the woman and her particular needs. True, a fancy Vienna wine-tasting may require fancy pants—a harem outfit, perhaps. And skirts can display to advantage a fetching ankle, shapely calves. Moreover, I'm aware that some women find trousers unsuitable, showing too much the padding around the hips and buttocks. (Others, it seems, want to show their upholstery.) Wide hips remain wide, skirt or no; but a jacket, whether a tailored garment or an unconstructed, loose one, can help. To each her own, I'd say—as is now largely the case.

Earlier, I touched on the topic of feminine roles. As a child, I rejected the very notion of dolls. Any that came my way was shelved, except a Raggedy Ann, a gift, which I tolerated as a decoration in my room. A homemade doll house, fashioned from a wooden orange crate, was accepted one Christmas, however, because I liked its miniature furnishings. I like small things and am interested in design. A favorite destination for me in days when I traveled to Chicago was the display of miniature rooms in the Art Institute.

Only a large golden Teddy Bear, with its beautiful coat and masculine name (and pronouns), found favor in my affections. He arrived the Christmas that I was five years old, I believe, in a handsome Teddy-sized pram made of green wicker. Sometime later I received as a gift *Pamela's Teddy Bears*, a clever British book for children, built around a little girl, assumed to be real, and the make-believe lives she invents for her bears.

Teddy survived in a storage cupboard in New Orleans for many years, but no longer was fit to display on my bed. That was remedied by a homestead (savings and loan association). It had advertised an attractive rate of interest on savings. With some disposable funds, I took the streetcar downtown and went in. My eye fell on a well-made stuffed tiger, with a smooth pelt and pleasant expression—a promotional gift for those depositing some minimum sum. He was, it turned out, the last of his kind—an endangered species indeed. Previous customers who got one probably took theirs home to their children; I was the child. Having left money in the bank's coffers, I took the tiger and cradled it in my arms as, uninhibited, I rode the streetcar home—a sight to locals and tourists alike, doubtless. I named the princely animal Lord Clive of India, but familiarly he is known as Mike the Tiger, like the mascot of LSU.

You must understand I did not and do not rebel; I *resist*. Or am I just contrarian? (The reviewer Patrick Henry identified a strong contrarian streak in *The Shimmering Maya and Other Essays*.) Well, there's a lot to be contrarian about. Resistance remains my watchword. Thus, under my eventual acceptance of the surface lay, and lies still, a deep conviction, more like an instinct, that what's *behind* appearances is what counts. But to pay dress service to norms is not hypocrisy; respecting that inner truth, one can still attend to the outer self as a courtesy to others. Manners are akin to morals, taking the prevailing mores into consideration. Properly understood, they are not a cover-up, a means to conceal the true self or its achievements by plagiarism, prevarication, or simple unawareness of one's failings.

Doesn't everyone have ontological confidence and a strong will to be oneself? No. Think back on what you have read of Kafka's childhood. An extreme example, to be sure. But I know someone whose father called him to his face a "worm." You can imagine the conflicts when my will met the world. No full-blown tantrums, as I recall, even when I was little, but firm resistance and, sometimes surely, shouting, maybe tears. I resisted particularly what I shall call "personal appropriation." I did not consider myself fodder for middle-aged women to exclaim and paw over—I was not a toy nor an interactive exhibit. I let them know it, too. Oh, my poor mother!

Oh, perhaps I did rebel! Nothing serious, you understand. In my girlhood my hair was fine, straight, and very black (like my Celtic grandmother's). I wore pigtails much of the time; or Mother used a curling-iron on me. Such curls did not last. As I left childhood for adolescence, it was impressed on me that curls of some sort were almost *de rigueur*—not at the Flying-G, not at home, but elsewhere. In Alpine High School days, I got very weary of curling irons and curlers but did not want to undergo a "perm." One day I took the scissors to my bangs where they fell over my forehead, producing a sort of buzz-cut. My rough model was that of a young camp counselor, married to a ranger from the Carson National Forest and of a practical nature. Did my mother have in mind moments like that when, many years later, she said, "It's surprising you turned out as well as you did"? (I took it as a compliment.)

My mother was horrified; my father paid no mind to the turmoil. When the short hairs grew out, I did not trim them again. Instead, at the end of my senior year, I created a Brunhilde coiffure consisting of two braids crossed on top of my head. My cousin Jean wore her hair in that style for many years and was the more beautiful for it. Whether it suited me I cannot say, really. What's certain is that it was in style nowhere I went. Finally, in my freshman year at Rice, the braids were replaced by an ordinary cut. Then I was back to curlers, of course.

In the course of time, the sense of extended family to which I alluded as having legitimacy as judges has expanded greatly to include wide circles of others, sometimes unseen. Likewise, the spirit of charity in me has expanded. Children are not known for their charity; some are little monsters, and even the best must be preoccupied with their own growing and learning. Nowadays, would I wish to offend my kind hosts who take me to dinner at a good restaurant by appearing in an old sweater with a hole in the sleeve, and with hair uncombed and no makeup? Or by using vulgar language? Heavens, no! Don't I wish to please the audience when I read poems at a literary powwow? Don't I wish for them to be well received?

The tomboy matter, mentioned in chapter three, is crucial. The stance was genuine; it was how I reacted to the world and its demands. I was not passive, philosophically; I had drive. As the boys I knew were preparing to assume roles in which they would shape the world, I too wanted to adopt a life of doing, of making. (The word *poet* comes from the Greek for *maker*.) Hence I preferred, to that of my own sex, their company; later, men's. That familiarity has served me in later life. I felt comfortable with both and have flattered myself that I understood them and what I shall call the male principle better than do most others of my sex. I resemble them, but not in every way. I've got a man's mind in a woman's body. I would not want to be any farther along on that spectrum, however; the notion of a powerful woman athlete is not appealing. I may not have tried sufficiently to understand one or two males (as they are now called) of my close acquaintance.

But I liked girls also, as different types of friends. It was usually with them that I hiked, biked, and played tennis. Part of my engagement during my happy weeks at the Flying-G was social. I did not know (nor at Rice, later) what homesickness was. I engaged easily in group endeavors in a spirit of teamwork. I like common goals, preferably without much overt competition. (In my 60s and 70s I still enjoyed camping out and vacations with teamwork or routine.) The point is not to beat others but to achieve together something all profit from. "To the top of the mountain!" But I was not tough physically nor dominating; such was ruled out by my slight build and my dislike of aggression. I am a sensitive woman, after all.[3]

A further word about the outdoors. I was at home in the mountains, which spoke to me in their beauty and majesty, their aroma and evening whispers, and called for energetic activity so that I could know them well. My love for trees dates likewise from that time; they often appear in my poetry. Valéry similarly found trees a superior creation of nature and wrote of them; Jean Giraudoux spoke of the "immobile brother of men" ("le frère immobile des hommes"). The Southwest desert lands where I camped as an adult similarly hold great beauties.

Following ninth grade in a Denver junior high school on a bizarre off-semester schedule, then one semester and a fraction at South High there, Alpine High School provided the remainder of my secondary school experience, The school was not a cradle of scholastic accomplishment, although a few students, with supportive families, did look ahead not only to a university education but to further training and a profession. The presence of Sul Ross ("The Athens of West Texas," joked my father), some 160 miles from any similar institution, gave the town prestige and attracted a few well-educated men and women who expected academic success from their sons and daughters. A scattering of students of my years went off to universities hundreds of miles distant, including an Ivy League institution. But college preparation was done quietly, without the fanfare and expenses accompanying pre-college grooming today.

Summers in Alpine were hot, dry, generally quiet. One police officer kept order in town; Sheriff Weber took care of law enforcement for the county, huge. He had a deputy or so on the river. Classes

---

[3]   See "Prospecting" in *The Shimmering Maya and Other Essays.*

were in session at Sul Ross, but I did not date college boys. Some high school students had jobs in town or on ranches—maybe their family's spread. A few may have gone to El Paso or Del Rio to work among kinfolk.

Others just lived. I was among them. Everyone my age drove, whether an old Studebaker or darling green Chevrolet for the teens or the family car. My father taught me after I turned fifteen: a few lessons on the Ft. Davis highway, study of a manual, and I had my license. We visited each other's houses, played canasta or gin rummy, took drives. Boys worked on those cars or their chemistry experiments. Four of us formed a vocal quartet. I practiced my flute, read, wrote (typing on the green Royal portable), and frequented the city library, a small collection launched and managed by Bonnie Newell, the sole Rice graduate in town. She was the wife of a businessman from the east, a Princeton graduate. Their son John, very intelligent, was my high school boyfriend. When a boy of his age became a ward of the county upon the death of his single father, the Newells took him in, treated him like a son, and sent him to an Ivy League school. His gratitude is marked by the name given to his first-born, "Newell Ann." (He also furnished a photograph for the present volume; the artist whose painting appears on the cover is his son.)

Summer travel with my parents to Colorado or elsewhere, starting when I was seventeen, provided much pleasure. Twice I went, driven by other parents, to a Methodist camp in New Mexico for a short stay. One summer I was a counselor for two weeks at a Girl Scout camp at Mitre Peak, to the northwest of Alpine; on another occasion, after my freshman year at Rice, thanks to a scholarship I spent two weeks at a camp on Lake Michigan.

The time with my family, on the road or at home, taught me the art and importance of conversation. "Conversation forms the mind," wrote Pascal. We sat in the living room, around the kitchen table, or outside, where we often had lunch or supper. Insects bothered us little; the phoebes and other birds took care of them. Inside, we tuned in to the noontime news on station KVLF, infamous (with us, at least) for the malapropisms distributed frequently by the announcers. We played three-handed bridge (my parents taught me the rudiments of the game) or listened to recordings of plays. We took drives west to Marfa, north to Ft. Davis, east toward Marathon and Ft. Stockton, or south through very rugged country toward Big Bend National Park. Pronghorns (called commonly *antelope*) were always visible to the east.

Alpine had two movie houses, the Grenada and the Toltec. The latter showed films in Spanish for Mexican-Americans. They went to the Grenada also, but, through convention, sat in the balcony. No signs, as I recall, pointed to this custom. On Saturday mornings my teenaged friends and I could see series of adventure films, some western, some African in the vein that H. Rider Haggard's thrilling *King Solomon's Mines* launched. The main fare was often a western, with Randolph Scott. My father would not enter the Grenada—too many germs floating around. But when two drive-in movie palaces were built on Highway 90, one on each side of town, we sometimes went for an evening, taking in such films as *Hans Christian Andersen*.

A reader may inquire, "What about the non-entitled, the non-leisured?" Some were Anglos (to use the term of the place and time, viewed as less offensive than "white"); most were "Mexicans," generally legal, I suppose, but some probably without papers. They were called on occasion "Latin-Americans" or by the name I have used above. Constituting about half of the population, they resided south of the Southern Pacific tracks. Unlike that in New Mexico, with substantial European elements forming a high class of Hispanics, the Trans-Pecos gene pool of Mexicans consisted mostly of native, that is, Indian blood. They all spoke Spanish most of the time. They were Roman Catholic; their church was on their side of the tracks, where the family of Dr. O'Donnell, certain members of the Newell family, and one other Anglo family, I recall, joined them on Sundays. Those who had jobs and those who attended school long enough generally had functioning spoken English. Some were illiterate in both languages. They did not have the advantages enjoyed by most Anglos, certainly not those of the better families.

Why not? Today's egalitarians blame class and economic differences solely on "white privilege." Consider, though, how many Mexicans did not complete high school when most could have, living at home; after-school or weekend jobs could have supplemented family income and still not interfered with attendance. The chief difficulty was that many of those students could not handle the material, or did not want to. It included American history and basic "civics" (facts about the U.S. and state constitutions), American and British literature (Shakespeare, notably), algebra, geometry, biology, chemistry, and physics. To the students of whom I write, much remained alien, even when teachers, trying to fill the culture gap, took into consideration the non-Anglo background from which they came.

The barrier was partly language, though not uniquely so. It thus went back to birth. Yet did most of those families not prefer to live in the USA rather than return to Los Estados Unidos de México, with no such language barrier? So they chose the Anglophone society but did not adapt to its culture. Thought and habits, including those of *machismo*, changed slowly. While many of the men did labor hard as ranch hands, gardeners, construction workers, and highway maintenance men, and others worked in stores, always a cohort, visibly unemployed, loitered in the daytime on the principal avenue (US 90), staring at Anglo women as they passed. Not a good example for the male youth. Meanwhile, the wives were sent out to work. We cannot change birth; we can offer opportunities. Not having chosen to be born nor selected their situation (family, sex, time), these men nevertheless were or should have been responsible for themselves and any children they engendered. The record was often sorry.

Readers will remember how, thanks to the presence of Professor Dowden and his wife in Alpine one summer, I was invited to apply to Rice. The application did not consist of much: two high school transcripts and his recommendation. I was accepted, on the condition that before matriculating I pass a trigonometry course. (Alpine's Miss Weyerts was doubtless able to teach the subject, but there was no call for it.) Rice charged no tuition at the time; I was even awarded a $200 scholarship for my first year. Every succeeding year I had support from one or another scholarship or prize fund. I arrived in Houston in late September of 1951 to begin my studies.

Coming from so far, knowing no other students, while most had graduated from Houston high schools and already had circles of friends, living in Rice apartments with a few other out-of-town girls, and on a very tight budget, I was without social advantages. But I joined a girls' "literary society" and other organizations, and eventually made many acquaintances among my classmates and others. One of these mates, Nancy Moore Eubank, was a friend and supporter of my endeavors for nearly seventy years. She and I took a winter cruise in the Gulf and Caribbean in January 2024. I regret very much to say that less than four weeks later she was dead.

Those four undergraduate years constituted a solid education, with nothing resembling a class Rice currently offers, dealing with Taylor Swift. My parents' conscientious labor at Alpine High and the high school in Marathon, then at Sul Ross, helped pay for that education and its associated pleasures. I did not think of trying to outdo fellow students; I wanted simply to do my best, as Evelyn understood. Still less would I have viewed a professor as competition or, like a rather juvenile graduate student of mine, attempted to show one up. True, I once noted to my math professor, known as Herr Reiter, that he had made an error—a simple slip—when writing on the blackboard; for him to go ahead on that figure would have led to difficulty. A gentleman, he thanked me graciously.

In addition to a grounding in three literatures, European history, and the required sciences and mathematics, I took two semester courses on the philosophy of education, to help prepare me for taking up my parents' trade. One summer, I registered for two classes at Sul Ross. They did not amount to much. Because the final examination period at Rice had not ended when the summer term began, I entered late. At my first class there was an exam. I made a grade in the high 90s. But the course was probably no worse than countless others in education curricula around the country; better than some, doubtless.

Had I been unable to afford further studies in French after graduation, I could have gotten a Texas certificate and a position teaching high school French, Spanish, history, or English, in the Trans-Pecos region or elsewhere. I would have set aside money and then, helped by an assistantship or fellowship, done advanced studies at Rice or at the University of Texas, and ultimately, Ph,D. in hand, taught at the college level. Such a counterfactual is without much interest; but it shows that I would have, determinedly, forged ahead.

My meeting with Patric Savage during the fall semester of my senior year made that detour unnecessary. We would marry and, supported by him and, subsequently, assistantships, I would pursue graduate studies at Rice. Representatives from the English and history departments solicited my application, but again, as when I was invited to major in history, I remained wedded to French and have never regretted it.

How could I? I like nearly everything France offers: a splendid (if odd) Latinate language that greatly enriched our own Anglo-Saxon speech (the result of wars, that is, an invasion and centuries of rivalry between two monarchies); beautiful fields and vineyards, seacoasts, and mountain scenes; one of the two greatest modern literatures; architecture and art that have been the marvels of the world; fine music from all periods; philosophy; and the greatest outdoor display of monumental structures in the world, the City of Lights. I enjoyed my teaching career tremendously and found meaning in it over forty years (if I count from my first teaching assistantship).

I must tackle further questions of my adult personality, some of which are connected directly to poems and prose of mine. If anyone wishes to call me neurotic, or supposes, upon reading the previous chapters, that I am, I shall not resist the term. I use it myself. Phoebe Elliott Hill may perhaps be thought of that way. And of course, my father was neurotic. He tolerated, for instance, no strange foodstuffs. "Strange" meant more or less everything his mother had not served. My neuroses include the restlessness he suffered and a lifelong horror of exotic foods and even certain plain ones. If at seventy or beyond one is not a bit neurotic, there's something wrong!

The truth is that my relationship to foodstuffs is what certain literary critics would call *problematic*. Excepting deviled eggs, preferably prepared by me, with pickle relish and well-seasoned, I won't eat anything where the egg (think of it: a chicken foetus, with incipient feathers!) is not disguised to the eyes and the taste. Custards are banned. Similarly, I am disgusted by oatmeal or anything like porridge. Bread pudding is out. I don't like even the word *pudding*. Any soft or runny cheese is *verboten*; only hard, firm, or crumbly cheese, such as blue, is acceptable. I do not like root vegetables much, although my grandmother did; what else would nineteenth-century Canadians have had in wintertime? I eat only muscle meat—no organs—and do not tolerate fat. I avoid cream sauces and gravies, especially white. Rather than risk being obliged to eat any of those outlawed foodstuffs at a restaurant or dinner party, I announce ahead of time or when the menus are distributed my various dislikes. Not very suave, right? But those with allergies may trumpet them, going so far sometimes as to describe the rash they got or a worse after-effect. When I decline gastronomic offers, whether delicacies or no, I am told, "Oh, but you'll like it *this* time." No, I shall not.[4]

Yet raw oysters are a favorite! Is that because I experienced them first at age seventeen and had no prejudice against them? After arriving in Houston to begin studies at Rice, I was taken to a famous seafood place and introduced to oysters on the half-shell as well as crab meat and shrimp—all pleasing, right away. Poems of mine on seafoods show them in favorable light, in contrast to foods I have mentioned above and a special object of dislike, portobello mushrooms. One deals with embodiment as one can.

Not displayed in society is my neurotic approach to bedding. I do not like duvets, "comforters," eiderdowns, or bulky quilts. With them, it's all or nothing at all. That's the European style, especially in the Germanic nations. In my luggage there's always a woolen throw. My prejudice is not unique; Queen Elizabeth II shared it, demanding

---

[4] See "Adventures in Food; or, the Ideal Meal" in *Music from the Lake and Other Essays* and food poems in several collections, e.g. on cheese and eggs.

wool blankets during her travels through the Commonwealth. This very day, a close friend told me that her husband likewise loathes such. Take them away! Wool blankets are the thing, pliable, lightweight, stackable, often washable—and giving employment to flocks of sheep around the world. But I don't refuse to lie down under a blanket of synthetic fibers.[5]

Added to my horror of duvets is my preference for narrow beds. Huge bedsteads are the standard now in all hotels I frequent. I have to put up such defenses as I can and suffer otherwise. I colonize a small area at the side of the mattress; I hurl onto the floor, or possibly behind a large chair, out of sight, most of the hotel bedding, including multiple unwanted pillows. (I like flat pillows. Why does the hotel furnish, along with neck rolls—of what use are they?—four heavy ones, unyielding to the head.) Then I spread out the throw and position myself carefully under it. Nor do I like today's mattresses. I do not want to sleep in or on a "pillowtop"; I want a firm surface with easily discernable edges from which I will not roll. Alas, one cannot (despite Christ's encouraging command to Lazarus) carry one's bed on a journey.

Why did we take up these duvets and other padded appurtenances? Such things were around during my childhood, but my parents and grandparents were not the only families with wool blankets and afghans. The army and navy used them. By the 1980s, I believe, duvets had begun to take over. The introduction of more, and cheaper, synthetic materials made them affordable, and they have become ever larger, with countless frou-frous, to accommodate today's huge beds and heavy bodies. Not very environmentally friendly, eh, since all that stuff is synthetic and, it has been shown, requires for manufacture more resources than fleece—the real one. Even cotton is no longer king. The chief reason for the duvet craze, though, is the sexual revolution: the extravagance of the duvet and its accessories apparently creates crests, hills, and valleys for pillow fights, rolling and dipping as at sea, playful suffocation, and other pleasures I know not of.

---

[5]   See the poem "Abed" in *On the North Slope.*

My taste for travel may be neurotic. Again, I think of Phoebe; I am truly her granddaughter. If not a compulsion, it is a need. The subtitle "A Life of Travels," imposed on me by the publishers for my essay collection *Finding Higher Ground*, does not fit everything in the book but cannot be considered inappropriate. Starting with my first trip, to Wyoming, with my mother, then the long drives to Edinburg and back, followed by a family postwar trip (1946, I believe) to the San Juans of Colorado, then the move to Alpine, I have often been taken on the road, and now I take myself, or by train or bus, in the air or asea. "Itchy feet" is the term.

A reviewer of *Journeying from Canyon de Chelly*, R. S. Gwynn, attacked it in the *Sewanee Review* for being too concerned with travel. Maybe he just didn't like what he knew of me. Maybe he couldn't go trotting here and there himself and bore resentment against one who could; or maybe he didn't want to, sticking closely to his region, the South. But why not tolerate the topic in others' poems? In the *Southern Review*, Donald Stanford highlighted, with approval, the emphasis on journeying. Poems of mine set in Catalonia, France, South America, or, closer to home, the American southwest, are among my most beautiful.

To travel is to experience aspects of the world beyond our daily ones. "Travels are the school of life," wrote Montaigne. True, one may learn a great deal from books also (he did, enormously), others' reports, paintings and drawings, still photographs, and films. Books offer keys to both present and past, which otherwise cannot be experienced. The beautifully printed art books that became affordable in mid-twentieth century popularized cultural treasures, as underlined by Malraux's idea of the "imaginary museum"; they have enriched millions. *National Geographic* magazine has offered topographic and ethnographic views to further millions. Still, seeing mountains rise at the horizon, feeling the tide on one's toes, visiting remote villages are experiences of a different order. And, in my case, there's simply the need to be elsewhere.

The poet Baudelaire, who was sent by his stepfather and mother (to separate him from his dissipated associates) around Africa as far as Reunion Island and Mauritius, wrote of the compulsion to get away. Among his most beautiful poems is "L'Invitation au voyage," which evokes Holland but suggests also the exoticism of the Dutch East Indies. Are such great distances sufficient? Maybe one needs greater changes, taking us, as he expressed it in an English-language title, "Anywhere out of the world." No; I'll stick now to what someone described to my friend David Clinton as his preference: "over-developed countries."

In addition to what you may view as my compulsion to travel is the vector toward action, which I mentioned earlier. Workaholic, if you wish. Someone inquired recently what my hobbies were. I replied that I had none. Pressed, I acknowledged that I did have a pastime or so: reading, the piano keyboard, crossword puzzles, and bridge. That's quite adequate, and perhaps others don't have many more; but none holds me ahead so well as research and writing.

Earlier I wrote of inhibitions. In that regard I note the utility of alcohol. No controlled drugs, though, ever; I prefer my pleasures to be legal. My father rarely took a drink; he told me that it was good he did not. Perhaps he knew that his body was not strong enough to endure it. Or did he sense in himself, vaguely, the risk of becoming too dependent on it? My cousin Sarah Vesty (daughter of Jean and Dwight Miller) has stressed the number of alcoholics in the family. No doubt, Edward, the archivist, was one. He was an introvert to start with, maybe a bit autistic. With a B.A. and M.A. in history from the University of California–Berkeley, he was drafted into the army at the time of the Korean War. In combat he lost an eye and two fingers. Afterward he joined the National Archives and worked more or less out of sight. He liked music and art and had friends, mostly fellow archivists, marrying one eventually. His personality was, however, peculiar. He died of cirrhosis of the liver before he was sixty. I do not know of others; ignorance may be a blessing. I have not been a victim.

I am also a terrible snob. I prefer intellect to obtuseness, learning to ignorance, about which I rage silently, refinement to vulgarity, and elevated language to low, both in English and French. (The French also make mistakes, despite the dictates of their Académie.) My former students may join me in language snobbery. Oh, it doesn't show often because I control it. The true elite of my world know and respect their tongue and want others to do likewise. I have corrected a doctor on occasion, when she wanted me to "lay down"; she now remembers that I did so, and smiles pleasantly when I remind her. I can do so courteously by noting that she surely hears the error everywhere. I correct waiters. I mark through mistakes in grammar and usage in the *Wall Street Journal*. Frequently I repeat in conversation what someone has said but in an altered form, showing, for example, how to avoid the double negative. "You said you didn't see *anything* there?" The tactic does not work; the error recurs within a few minutes. The offenders don't realize they've been rebuked, and I am not viewed as a pretentious pedant, since they don't know the word—nor the expression they might apply to me otherwise, "harmless drudge," Samuel Johnson's definition of a scholar.

You understand that I do not expect many of my fellow Americans to know the poetry of Baudelaire, Apollinaire, and Valéry, the long masterpiece by Proust. (Ipso facto, to know them is to be superior.) One might expect, however, that any American with a bachelor's degree would know where Genoa is and be able to name the two petroleum capitals of the U.S. More generally speaking, I detest what is vulgar. Of course I realize that good character does not require correct grammar, and many people who are ignorant of proper speech or don't realize its importance for culture have far more integrity and work much harder than literary snobs, "public intellectuals," and others in the "elite" category. I cannot scorn anyone who works honorably at a useful trade and contributes to family and social welfare, I do not make those around me suffer much from my attitude; most of them don't even recognize it. But if we are to have culture—that is, the high culture of Western civilization—it must be fostered. We must recognize it, maintain it, contribute to it, and pass it on.

Unlike my father, partly through both nature and luck, partly doubtless because of my parents' vigilance while I was a girl, I have been fortunate to be well and strong and have enormous vitality. They shared concern for my health and well-being. Exercise in fresh air was abundant. During the rationing regime of World War II, which provided very limited amounts of protein, sugar, and fat, Mother endeavored to feed me as well as my peculiar preferences would allow. For years I was given a preparation called Myeladol, made now by Upjohn, composed of cod liver oil, malt, and added vitamins and minerals, in a molasses-like preparation. The aftertaste was not welcome. No matter.

Thanks to this vitality, I have been able, despite inborn craving for new experiences, to enjoy stability, productivity, and a generally active life. Since Kate's birth, I've spent no night in a hospital. True, I had non-Hodgkins lymphoma in 2017. Why? Readers will see in due course what my responsibilities were at that time. Worry, day after day; not much sleep, night after night. Strains. Since my mind was not going to buckle, the body did. I am grateful to the good doctor in charge of my care and all those behind her whose research and sometimes sufferings (as human subjects) made possible the drugs, potent, though damaging, that cured me.

What is the good life? The Greeks asked that question. Aristotle asserted that no one can be considered happy until his death, the only certain indication that thenceforth things cannot go horribly wrong. For years, Oedipus enjoyed a very good life, with a devoted wife, children, and a royal position. His example warns us against the inclination we might have to "go with the preponderance of the evidence." Still, we do incline in that direction; we must, in order to save sanity. Or we take the comparative approach: "We are certainly better off than many." Or "There but for the grace of God go I." Indeed. But God's grace may wane or cease. Still, as Meursault (in *L'Etranger*, by Camus), who is in prison and faces a death sentence—thus close to the end Aristotle required—discovers, "I had been happy and I still was."

At least I know good fortune when I see it and live it, as so often I have done.

Chapter Eight

Marriage and Graduate Studies

Patric Savage (1928-2017) and I married as I was about to graduate from Rice. He had been drafted into the army shortly after receiving his Bachelor of Arts degree in 1952, with a major in mathematics. He might have been posted to Korea. But, seeing that among his credentials were two years of German at Rice, the authorities sent him to West Germany, next door to Soviet-controlled territory. Discovering then that he was not skilled as an interpreter— he had not claimed to be—the army assigned him to a construction battalion in eastern France, where he spent eighteen months. With his knowledge of mathematics and draughtmanship, his service was highly useful. He learned a good deal of French, studying on his own as well as acquiring conversational skills in local bars and among families who invited him in.

His discharge in hand, he returned to Rice in September 1954 to embark on graduate studies. Our first encounter was in the library, on the steps going up to the second floor. An auspicious beginning, an appropriate sign—since in our separate and joint lives books played an enormous role. He also worked full-time at Hughes Tool Company. He was handsome, personable, and very intelligent; in addition, he resembled Aunt Flora and my father—that Irish sense of humor. He and Aunt Flora got along marvelously well. Both were

Patric Savage and Catharine Hill,
Alpine, January 1st, 1955

full of vitality; both, having been deprived of a full childhood, were determined to draw from life as much as possible and to give life their best.

There was no money in his background. His parents had wed sometime after World War I, when his father, known as Jack, was discharged from the American army, his lungs close to ruined from mustard gas. Born in 1893 in County Dublin, Ireland, he had left home and arrived in Massachusetts in 1909. To gain his American citizenship, he joined up in 1917. After the war, having resettled in St. Louis, he worked in the grocery business and married; but he was not well. Pat's mother, Elvira, was born (1900) in America shortly after her parents and the older children immigrated from Denmark.

Half Irish and half Danish, thus, though not a melancholy Dane, Pat was christened Charles Robert but called by everyone "Paddy." As a young adult he replaced his birth name by Patric (and no middle name), a spelling choice that underlined his individuality. A sister was born four years later, a brother later.

During most of the 1930s Jack Savage underwent treatment for tuberculosis, at one time in a Colorado sanitarium, later in a Veterans' Hospital. Elvira worked at various jobs. Depression-era salaries being low and unemployment lines long, she may have considered herself lucky to get anything. I think that relatives must have helped with child care. Pat spent fifteen months in a boarding school-cum-camp for children of tuberculars. Jack returned home from time to time, escaping once from a facility. The family lived quite marginally, in rented quarters. In one house, they shared a bathroom. In another—the worst—the flat had cold water only and the sanitary facilities consisted of an outside latrine over a concrete channel that the city flushed hourly. Pat waited in bread lines sometimes, and Elvira scrubbed floors to earn a pittance until an uncle of hers gave her a waitress job at his railroad station restaurant.

Jack died in January 1939, when Pat had just turned ten. Elvira's pension as a war widow was next to nothing. He was thus thrust into a role, called then "man of the house," for which his father had not been able to prepare him. From age fourteen he had at least part-time employment. An early job was as a deckhand. (Pat became a great admirer of Mark Twain and collected numerous editions of his works.) There was still barely enough money to get by, even after Elvira found a position with the Civil Aeronautics Administration.

Pat broke with religion shortly after his father died. While his mother was an Episcopalian from an odd Danish sect, his father was, of course, Roman Catholic, and Pat was not only a pupil in Holy Family Parish School, where he attended mass every morning, but a choir boy. The Roman layers he had accumulated were deep and weighty. But as I have written, he was highly intelligent. At his father's funeral, a cleric of some sort told him to say a string of Hail Marys and other prayers, which would purportedly get his father out of purgatory. The fellow had not counted on the boy's knowledge. Belief was an edifice, all parts interdependent. When one failed, the whole system collapsed.

The family moved to St. Charles, Missouri, where Pat attended high school. After graduation, he spent a year at Missouri School of Mines, but his mother could not afford to support him further. He found work at a St. Louis brewery, to which he commuted by bus, and then was hired by American Car and Foundry in St. Charles, where his design ability earned him promotions. When the Naval ROTC launched a campaign for applications, he applied and was selected, then assigned to Rice. He did not arrive there, so to speak, on a turnip truck. His brilliant mind, experience, and reading provided him with ample credentials. But he was obliged to live in rented rooms, husbanding his funds, working every summer, traveling to Houston by bus. He remained in the program for two and a half years, until a serious misjudgment led to loss of that financial ticket. He began working full-time at Hughes and became eligible for the draft following graduation.

In 1952 Hughes was pleased to have him back. Building on what he had done with record-keeping, he transformed the entire inventory—categories of rock bits and individual specimens—by computerizing them. He would eventually specialize in mass data storage on the giant computers of the era. But juggling his graduate studies, which I endorsed, of course, with his full-time work at Hughes ultimately proved impossible. After two years he left the program.

Meanwhile, I had my own pursuits, with enormous reading lists. Rice's Ph.D. program in French was quite new and somewhat understaffed; but the training, especially in literary history, was solid. He and I worked long days, Pat putting in extra hours, both always striving for excellence. Starting my second year, I had a teaching assistantship. Study was both intellectual endeavor and career preparation but never pastime. As for poetry, it was a similarly serious matter for me—never a hobby, never an adornment or decoration. I am no "Sunday poet" (by analogy with "un peintre du dimanche" or "Sunday painter"). Pat managed to play tennis frequently, I'm pleased to say. He made sacrifices for me and my career, the chief living as a bachelor while I was in France on a Fulbright fellowship (1957-1958). The fellowship allowed me to work on Gide and study with authorities on such authors as Apollinaire and Stendhal. I am grateful for his enthusiastic support.

We designed such free time as we had together for companionship. We had friends connected to Rice and Hughes. We attended lectures at Rice, musical performances, and art film showings. Small clusters of students came to our apartment on Vassar Street, and we were invited to the faculty club at Rice and the home of my dissertation director, André Bourgeois. And we were able to enjoy road trips, some to visit our family members elsewhere. One took us to Canada, via St. Louis, where we visited Pat's mother, and the upper Mississippi River valley, into Saskatchewan and Alberta. Returning, we drove south through Montana and Wyoming to see Colorado relatives, then through New Mexico to Alpine, and eventually home. For Pat, the trip was a professional one, with visits on behalf of Hughes to oilfields and offices in Calgary and Edmonton. We made it a camping adventure also, staking out appealing spots in forest locations to which we could drive, then concealing the car among trees and making our bed on the needles of conifers.

On another occasion, we spent time in Mexico, I having ridden down to the capital in the car of my Fulbright friend Nancy Hoy McCahren and her husband, Mick, who was to study law there, then Pat driving down to join us and take me back. Before returning we visited states on both coasts and in between. We saw Veracruz, Cuernavaca, and villages, ate strange things (not entirely to my taste), stopped in cathedrals, churches, and museums in Mexico City, and tumbled in the waves off Acapulco. All was better then; or was it just that we were young?

André Bourgeois (1902-1994) was my professor in certain nineteenth-century French literature courses and two on Molière and Racine. He was not, originally, my dissertation supervisor. I was to work under the direction of Professor M., as I call him. Noticeably exophthalmic, he was considered brilliant; his mind ran to the abstract and the obscure. He was also inattentive to time, keeping his seminar students for an hour or more after the class was to end. It was he who, ruling out other twentieth-century subjects I proposed, assigned me the topic of Gide's religious thought. You may have supposed that my long study of Gide, which produced books and innumerable articles and is reflected in an earlier chapter, was a personal choice. No; it was imposed upon me. Why that subject? Did Professor M. know how well the man, writing, thought would suit me? A prospectus, with outline, was approved, and, in fall 1959, I began writing. At the same time, I was taking two graduate seminars and teaching first- and second-year French classes.

One morning in October, Professor Bourgeois came to my library carrel to tell me that he would take over the direction of that work: Professor M. had left the university. Dr. Bourgeois cited as an explanation what must have been dictated by the administration for public distribution. He would not have been taken in. (In a similar cover-up, at Tulane, faculty members were ordered to recite, for a professor's sudden change in status, an official formulaic excuse and enjoined from saying anything else.) Having appreciated my new advisor's teaching and come to admire his character, I was not distressed. To his honor: he, who did not like Gide's works much, did not oblige me to drop the topic, as others might, for selfish reasons. He encouraged me, promptly read my chapters (written in French, against custom), offered corrections, and worked, essentially, at the same pace I did. I salute him.[1]

Very few years later, the shining moon under which Pat and I lived and loved became clouded. Why did we separate and then divorce? Insofar as he and I wished, later, to revisit our past, we concluded that the parting was due to what's called ambition. True enough, as far as it went. But how far was that? It would have been Pat's and mine, together—but then separately. Yet I was not ambitious in the sense in which the word is commonly used today. The full-page CNBC advertisements of 2023-2024 in the *Wall Street Journal* that urge us to "live ambitiously" leave me indifferent. There is a distinction between ambition and drive. To get ahead, displacing rivals, if that's what ambition means, may be impossible; there is almost always someone in front of us. My goal was to live, or, better, to *become* as I lived. That is a dynamic goal, deep-seated.

Nevertheless, what I agreed to is associated with ambition. It had already been demonstrated by my Fulbright year and two summers spent in Paris doing research and soaking up French intellectual culture, particularly drama. During those periods Pat worked long hours at Hughes and advanced his reputation. Perhaps those absences, productive in their way, were nonetheless harmful. In 1962-1963 I was willing for us to separate again for an academic year in order that I might go to the East Coast and investigate what I supposed, erroneously, were better opportunities, or doorways to them. I had been influenced by criticism of the academic inbreeding indicated on my résumé; parochialism was looked upon with great disfavor, and I wanted to rectify it. From someone older and more familiar with the academic scene elsewhere I received very poor advice. He projected onto me his own wishes to resettle, away from Houston, which he did not like. (He missed the museums, the bookstores, the many musical performances, and the baseball of

---

[1]   See "New Orleans: The Winter Hour" in *Places in Mind*.

New York. Retrospectively, I feel for him.) For his part, Pat followed the beckoning of fate to what seemed to be an excellent position on the opposite coast, in California.

These new situations were to be launching pads for a rendezvous and positions side-by-side elsewhere. He could not know that by going to California to work for a defense contractor he was stepping into a trap, one aspect of which can be summarized as "last in, first out." That simplistic thinking sounds equitable but may be a disadvantage for the corporation. Certainly, his employer lost a brilliant man. The heads at a second huge corporation erred in assigning him to a major project that he deemed unrealizable. He said so. They were unappreciative, not recognizing the value of frankness and, worse, his enormous potential for the future.[2]

One must conclude that we did not use our freedom well. Sartre, who did not believe in God, nevertheless offered insight into the Almighty, arguing that He loved freedom more than morality; unable to make man both free to choose and yet predetermined as good, He made him free.

Here I shall lap ahead in this narrative by forty-four years. It is sometime in the winter of 2007-2008. Pat and I are in a Houston restaurant with my old classmate from Rice, Tom Biggs, and his wife, Katherine. We are all elated; the event is to celebrate the wonderful reconnection of the Savages, after that long separation. In just a few months we will be remarried. Following casual exchanges, Tom and Katherine inquire, directly, "But why did you split up?" As one, we replied immediately, "We don't know." Was it Karma, Providence, Fate, that force I have mentioned here and examined in many poems? Perhaps. Yet we wondered how we could have undone that which had been, we thought, so well done.

Do you, my readers, believe in Fate? I have addressed the subject before. Many of us have witnessed unusual manifestations of chance, a chance that served our purposes by amazing coincidence, or instead disserved them, thwarting us with apparent malignity. A

---

[2]   On the break-up, see the "Postface" in *Breakwater.*

Houston friend of mine went as a young woman to Central Asia and the Indian subcontinent. She was frequently alone, though she did travel with other Westerners sometimes, hitchhiking or riding with a group in an old, coughing vehicle. (In Iran, she noted the terrible aggression towards her of males, who grabbed at her person, even when she was accompanied by young men.) On the return journey, having made it back to Europe but entirely without funds to continue, she went to the American Express office in Amsterdam to wire her parents, New Yorkers. They too were traveling, in Spain; she had an address. Upon entering the office, she was amazed to espy them; some whim had made them abandon their Spanish stay to go to the Netherlands.

My longtime friend Patricia Teed, having lost one day a gold bracelet that had belonged to her grandmother, and having searched repeatedly her office, car, garage, and house, sent a desperate plea to the deceased ancestor and, by implication, to some obscure power. (Yet she eschewed entirely the Christian religion, finding that to believe in a tortured God, that is, Christ on the cross, was too much.) "Mommy Abbott, help me find my bracelet." The next morning, opening her car door, she saw it prominently displayed, like the jewel it was, in the center of the passenger seat. There are surely forces we know not of; some appear benign but others may be Jokers who take malicious pleasure in undoing us.

Yet I do not want to blame the failure of my first marriage on a malign force. A benign one, then, working through irregular, illogical ways? *Amor fati.* A strange dialectic, imitating the Christian one, would justify error—*felix culpa*, a Fall of sorts—in order that greater benediction, even redemption, might come about. As an adolescent seminarian in Algeria, his birthplace, my friend the writer Jules Roy heard one day by chance those very words pronounced by one priest to another, as they passed him in the cloister. The scales fell from his eyes; he apprehended, belatedly, the fact that he was an illegitimate son, placed in the seminary by his mother as atonement. (He did not remain there.) Between the two lives Pat and I lived together, he had a long, childless marriage to another woman who had been wed twice before him. He may have been a savior in her difficulties, chiefly poor health and poor judgment. I too married another, some years later, after my father's death, and produced a child. Through that child, Pat acquired a family when we remarried. An eighteenth-century poem by William Cowper underlines the unknowable ways of God, who "moves in a mysterious way / and rides upon the storm."

Ultimately, Pat and I simply took responsibility for doing the unwise thing. Following his death (August 2017), I penned these lines:

He wore his genius on his sleeve;

remember him, rejoice—yet grieve.

Genius refers to his exceptional mind but also his genie, his particular spirit, which his friends and in tennis circles recognized fully.

Regret has salutary properties. Recognizing error, we may try to mend our ways. We may attempt atonement. Ruefully, we may think of our loss as a strange opportunity, whereby we pay for previous blessings and perhaps earn future ones. Protestants, especially Calvinists, along with Catholic sects such as the Jansenists, have, historically, insisted that salvation cannot be earned; it is bestowed, perhaps even predestined; it is a grace. The poet Pierre Jean Jouve argued, more or less, that the gracious gift of salvation through Christ's suffering is exercised and valued ever more as need for it increases; in that case, let's all go out and sin! Without embracing it wholly, I am inclined toward the orthodox Catholic position, according to which good works and repentance are efficacious. Many of us know that we have erred and feel that we need to earn the forbearance, if not forgiveness, of others and God's benediction. We need to pay. "Let me do something for you," one says to a friend who has assisted us at some expense. "Everyone feels a little guilty," says Meursault in *L'Etranger*. We need to "give back." The regret is the acknowledgment and the punishment. As Edith Piaf, thinking doubtless of her own tumultuous life, her many tears, sang, "Il faut tant et tant de larmes / Pour avoir le droit d'aimer."

Following our separation, my six years in Virginia and Florida were pleasurable and favorable to my dual career as poet and French professor. (I did not settle in the Northeast, although positions were available. None offered marked advantages.) My first three scholarly books appeared, and I composed many poems that went into *Watering*, my first collection. Virginia offered proximity by car and train to major cities, starting with nearby Washington (where I went to musical events and exhibits with cousin Edward Hill, the archivist). Even visits to New York and Philadelphia were not impractical from Florida by train. I could enjoy museums, attend conferences, meet literary figures, and dine occasionally at a famous eatery.

At the University of Florida, colleagues were kind to me. A graduate student, Ilona Richey, became my friend; she and her husband took me out and about on more than one occasion. I was not invited into the chairman's social circle; perhaps there was none. He had hired me by correspondence after meeting me in Paris one summer. At the first departmental social event, his wife, having noticed me and learned who I was, was heard to say, "So this is what my husband brought back from Paris!"

Though teaching full loads and having to adjust to different campuses and college mores, I had time in those six years to read a great deal of American poetry and prose of the mid-twentieth century. Among the established authors I met and from whose work I profited were James Dickey and George Garrett, both already known to me from Rice (Dickey had been a neighbor in the Rice apartments), Howard Nemerov, and Flannery O'Connor. I was pleased to make the acquaintance, among the younger set, of James Seay, Henry Taylor, and Robert Wallace. An English professor at Florida, John Fain, a Vanderbilt product who had been close to the Fugitives, cultivated on his own a group of young scholars and poets in the hope of maintaining some of that historic Vanderbilt spirit.[3]

---

[3]   See the poem "Dickey at Rice" in *Under the Pergola*.

The landscapes, seascapes, and climates in both Florida and Virginia were of continual interest to me—three coasts and many beaches in Florida, all somewhat different from each other, along with forests, springs, deep pools, and islands; in Virginia, Tidewater coasts and islands, mountains westward. Historic properties and sites caught my attention; some were nearly at my front door. The libraries at the University of Florida and UVA were sufficient for most of my research needs. I got a modest grant to support one month of residence on the shore south of St. Augustine to write poems, of which most, along with additional verse, appeared in *Watering*.

I left the southeastern region despite its appeal. Perhaps the artist's instinct told me that I had drawn from it as much as I wanted, or required. Artists are needy, even predatory. I had borrowed the territory but it was not mine; I was a westerner, with some southern experience. In fall 1967 I decided to look at positions in French advertised elsewhere. The Tulane position caught my eye. It was time to return to the Gulf Coast and stay there.

Chapter Nine

New Orleans and New Marriage

At the 1967 December MLA convention in Chicago, I met faculty members from Tulane University, including Paul William Brosman, Jr. (1927-2010). When I was invited for an interview on campus, I was put up at the Pontchartrain Hotel and taken to dinner at old Etienne's, on Maple Street. (Years later, the Bayou Bar at the Pontchartrain became a watering place for me and friends, along with The Columns Hotel.)

New Orleans, founded in 1718, has prestige as the oldest major city in the Louisiana Purchase, unique in the United States. Until 1862, the principal language was French; and it had its own literature. The Spanish element, dating from the eighteenth century, contributed to the European foundation and the enduring foreign flavor. Officially, France still views the city in a proprietary fashion. During a state visit, De Gaulle spoke of his pleasure in setting foot on "French territory."

Neither too small nor too large, Tulane had a Ph.D. program in French and—as I found out—very solid library holdings, many bound in red leather in the series "Les Grands Ecrivains de la France." Research was expected and supported; but, in the French and Italian department, classroom teaching likewise was deemed important, since basic language courses, well taught, may lead students to

Paul W. Brosman, Jr.

choose upper-level classes as electives and perhaps declare a major or minor. The university struck me thus as compatible with my character, and my qualifications suited it.

Yet it might have been otherwise. Two previous candidates for my position had been interviewed on campus and had received attractive offers, but each had declined the chance to come: one, because his demand that his wife get a job in the German department was not met; the other, because at a reception given for him, the husband of a French faculty member said such awful things about the schools in New Orleans that the candidate was frightened off. I had no spouse to place; I had no children. These are the contingencies I wrote of in connection with my father; thus does Fate operate.

New Orleans could have been, however, merely a short stop on a continued journey around American and Canadian universities. For in academe, the 60s constituted a seller's market. During the initial months at Tulane, I was approached by the University of Oregon, Washington University (St. Louis), and UCLA. The last was especially interested in my qualifications and urged me to visit the campus. I declined. Had I wanted to move to the University of Waterloo, Canada, where I taught in summer 1970, I would have been invited. My liking for the Crescent City and the university were good reasons to remain.

Paul Brosman, Sr., the father of the man I married, was not a southerner, though nearly so. He was born in Albion, in southern Illinois, where his father owned the drugstore and also practiced dentistry, having obtained his diploma from the University of Missouri. The Brosman family antecedents were in the German counties of Pennsylvania and, before that, the Rhineland. Paul, Sr. did three years of undergraduate work at the University of Illinois and took a law degree there. Having decided by then, however, that he wanted to teach the law, not practice it, he needed to get a B.A. degree, expected of a future professor. For that purpose, he went to Indiana University for a fourth undergraduate year. There he and Katherine Lewis, called Kate, who was finishing her degree, met and married, in 1925, I believe. She was a distinguished woman. I recall being introduced to her in her large condominium apartment on St. Charles Avenue at Jackson. She received me graciously. I liked her immediately, and we came to understand each other well.

She was a native of Georgia, born in 1902 in Fitzgerald. Her grandfather was an Alsatian named Loos, who had landed in Savannah shortly before war broke out in 1861 and was drafted into the Confederate army. Captured by Union forces, he was imprisoned in Indiana. There, the presiding officer learned that the prisoner, whose name had been changed by an immigration official, was a pastry cook of note; the prisoner became a Unionist. Following the war, he remained in the north initially but at some date resettled in Georgia. It must be a son of his who became the father of Katherine.

Paul, Sr., was hired by the law school at Mercer University. A year after the birth of their only child, the young couple went to New Haven so that he could get a master's in law. When Rufus Harris, of Mercer, was appointed dean of the law school at Tulane, he hired his former Mercer colleague. Thus Paul Jr. became a New Orleanian not long after his birth. Except for his time in the Marine Corps and four years at the University of North Carolina, he never lived elsewhere. Traveling once to Colorado with me during our marriage and visiting Alpine twice were nearly more than he could endure.

As a boy and young man, Paul, Jr. was called "Pete," to distinguish him from his father, and the name stuck. I used it some but preferred, ultimately, his father's and my father's name. He almost surely had Asperger's syndrome, unidentified, of course. His parents recognized that something was amiss; he did not speak until age three, and he rocked far too much, too seriously, one might say, in a little chair that they had purchased for him. Consultations with doctors were unproductive. His mother told me that giving birth to that child was nothing; rearing him was another matter. The rocking habit remained with him always. Certain other traits on the Asperger's spectrum became obvious later. One can start with his difficulty in dealing with anything new. Familiarity was essential; order likewise. In addition, he experienced unease in most social situations. In his youth, I was told, having been invited by the parents of a young woman he was to take out to wait in the parlor, he wrote his name on a dusty table. He found it awkward to meet strangers and was not at ease conversing even with his colleagues. In contrast, he spoke easily to people in bars, inviting them home on occasion for long evenings (testing my endurance). Clearly, he did not feel threatened by the typical bar patron in New Orleans, whose local accent did not match his (soft, slightly Southern) and whose intellectual scope was far from his. Not that he boasted or showed off his learning; it would have been lost on them anyhow.

He believed ill luck followed him. Yet he was of good birth, attended Newcomb Nursery School and, for twelve years, Metairie Country Day School, was in good health, quite handsome, and close to six feet in height (he played basketball in high school). He was not without friends; he belonged to a high school fraternity, then Sigma Chi at Tulane. Moreover, he had courted and married a woman he loved. The union produced no children.

His wife, née Margaret Cuneo of New Orleans, and he were classmates. He majored in French, carrying on the language he had studied at Country Day; she chose Spanish as her major. On the advice of his father, who foresaw another conflict not long after World War II, he enrolled in the Naval ROTC to avoid a likely draft. But a summer training cruise revealed a deep antipathy toward the ocean; so he became a Marine. In 1949 he received his bachelor's degree in French; in 1950, a master's degree and his lieutenant's commission.

That was when he married, in June, the same month in which the North Koreans crossed the 38th parallel. He was sent immediately to Quantico, Virginia, for further training and then to Korea. Having for air travel the same dislike he had for sailing, he chose to travel to his next assignment, Camp Pendleton, California, by bus. In El Paso, between busses, he crossed on foot the bridge to Ciudad Juárez. Upon returning, he found his right back pocket slashed. Nothing was missing, however; being left-landed, he did not keep his wallet there. That was a bit of luck. By a much greater good fortune, he was not wounded. He served honorably on the Board of Awards and did his time in foxholes and the cold.

Readers who remember the politics of winter 1988 will take interest in testimony he gave in court that season as a witness in a suit brought against Pat Robertson, the charismatic Evangelical Christian broadcaster, a former fellow Marine in Korea and a major candidate for president in the Republican Super Tuesday primaries. Robertson's father, a Virginia senator, had been unable to keep his son out of combat entirely, but had seen to it at least that he received special treatment. The suit was brought by a Republican Congressman from California, Paul "Pete" McCloskey, Jr., likewise a Marine, who recruited others to join him in testifying. McCloskey argued that the popular broadcaster was unfit for office by reason of his character. Paul and others testified that he had frequented prostitutes and brought back liquor, condemned by his voting bloc, from generous leaves in Japan. In turn, Robertson sued McCloskey, but the suit was thrown out. The testimonies were publicized nationally before the primaries; the campaign fell apart.

The coincidence of Paul's commissioning and the North Korean invasion surely struck him as ill-fated. But he survived the war, and, having investigated the three universities with graduate programs to suit him—California at Berkeley, Yale, and North Carolina—he applied to the last of these, and, being accepted, settled with Margaret in Chapel Hill. She worked on a Ph.D. in Spanish; he embarked on one in comparative historical Indo-European linguistics, specializing in Old Germanic and Old Romance and, of course, with the required foundation in Sanskrit, Greek, and Latin. He would later work on Hittite. For a year or two he taught concurrently at North Carolina Central College.

Worse than the war on a personal level, indeed terrible, was the automobile accident in Denton, Texas, where in 1956, Ph.D. in hand, he had accepted an assistant professor's position to teach French, his graduate minor, at North Texas State. With his credentials, he would have been more suited to a university with graduate programs in his fields. In fact, he did get such an offer from Cornell University. But it arrived in the mail the day after he had accepted the North Texas position. Having given his word to take the Texas job, he could not, of course, go back on it. Why the Cornell offer did not come earlier, or why he did not wait longer for a response, is unknown.

The night of the accident, Margaret was at the wheel, as usual. Paul did not drive. In his teen years, someone, perhaps his mother, tried to teach him; possibly he even got a license. But, having driven into Bruno's Bar on Maple Street, which was not a drive-in bar, he may have decided not to experiment any further; or maybe others decided for him. On the night of the unfortunate occasion in Denton, Margaret, who was diabetic, had a black-out. Paul, though in the "Death Seat," was unhurt. She, in contrast, received lifetime injuries, being paralyzed from the neck down and losing much of her former ability to reason and remember. A terrible fate indeed. He remarked to me that it would have been better for them both to die.

She was hospitalized in Denton; Paul continued teaching there. In 1957, he moved her to New Orleans, where he obtained an appointment at the newly opened LSUNO (presently the University of New Orleans). Margaret spent months in care facilities, including the New Orleans Home for Incurables, and was flown for operations elsewhere. In other periods, in better or worse condition, she and Paul lived in a modest double (a two-storied half-house) on Panola Street with her widowed mother, who worked for the Louisiana Wildlife and Fisheries Department. Mrs. Cuneo did not drive; busses and streetcars were her transportation. She got supplies at French Quarter markets or at corner grocery stores.

Margaret was in a hospital bed, downstairs. Paul slept on a cot in the same room. He was her only caretaker in the evenings and at night. Five days a week he was replaced in the daytime by an untrained but devoted caregiver named Alice Johnson. Until 1965, when, thanks chiefly to Professor Panos P. Morphos, he got an appointment at Tulane, located nearby, he took three busses every weekday to get to the LSUNO campus, where he usually had 8:00 classes, owing to a sadistic, man-hating department head and her cronies. At home, he graded papers, wrote his scholarly articles in pencil on yellow legal pads (he never learned to type), saw to Margaret's needs, smoked cigarettes, drank bourbon, and ate one meal a day in the evening at Compagno's Restaurant, around the corner.

The friends mentioned earlier, classmates and fraternity brothers, included William G. (Billy) Richards; the attorney Charles Dunbar and his brother George, the painter; V. L. Ewing; and Robin Hardy. They could do little for Paul during the years of Margaret's incapacity; no one could do much. Visitors to the Panola Street house, ill-suited to guests, were rare. After thirteen years of suffering, she died, and Paul and I were able to marry, these friends again became a circle for him. Thanks to them and to other acquaintances, we were invited to Mardi Gras balls, with call-outs; later, Paul became a member of the Boston Club, met friends there for lunch, and took me to the annual parties.

Another friend, to be called merely "Herb," was not quite in those social circles, though the men I have mentioned were acquainted with him. I give considerable space to his portrait for two reasons, its inherent interest and his unwelcome presence in my married life.

He had New Orleans roots and was a Tulane man but had moved away. His income was ample; he had lots of blue-chip investments. For years he taught finance on various southern campuses. He and his wife, Liz, were often in New Orleans, however, staying in their VW camper or, later, in their town-house, another investment. We saw them often at the Bright Star, a bar-restaurant at the corner of Panola and Burdette streets; it had replaced the Compagno's that we frequented earlier.

In Paul's Panola Street days, Herb and Liz, a little mouse of a woman, dropped in often, especially on weekends. As though unaware of the dismal surroundings, they would park themselves for hours, watching football, conversing (Herb was a talker, all right), and eating and drinking liberally. It is my understanding that at no time did they provide the wherewithal. They had, obviously, no sense of reciprocity. Once Herb reported to us his distress at realizing that new acquaintances in a town where he and Liz had recently settled did not, after the first weeks, continue to invite them to their dinner parties and backyard barbecues. He was puzzled. What had gone wrong?

Readers will find it difficult to believe that such a *pique-assiettes* could exist and be tolerated in modern times; he sounds like a character from an eighteenth-century French work such as *Le Neveu de Rameau* or a Victorian novel. I am not sure myself why he was not sent away. Paul might have preferred no company. But Herb came, at least, from the past, before the accident, and from that less remote past to which he must have clung as being familiar, however awful. After Paul and I married, Herb and Liz would come by, similarly unannounced, generally in early afternoon if it was a weekend day or at the end of the afternoon. Through deeply planted southern custom, Paul offered drinks and snacks. They would stay for hours. I think we never urged them to stay to dinner. My grocery lists were made out and meals planned for two adults and a daughter. I do not "whip up something" on the spur of the moment. I recall a prolonged cocktail-hour visit one December when my mother was with us. For a long while I postponed serving dinner, waiting out the unwelcome guests, successfully but at the expense of unhappy appetites.

Dear Readers, you see that Herb was a tightwad. You do not yet know the extent of his parsimony and its social expressions. He could out-miser many a miser, perhaps even Molière's Harpagon. Instead of subscribing to the local newspaper, he would fish out the previous day's edition from his neighbors' garbage can, a reliable depository. When those neighbors moved, he went to a certain McDonald's every morning because it provided a few copies for its clientele. He and Liz bought day-old bread at an outlet bakery and, at supermarkets, discounted meat. When Liz got cancer early in her sixties, Herb, who had not taken his Social Security at age 62, preferring to wait for a larger package at 65, urged her to postpone treatment for three years. This was the single occasion I know when she protested, that is, successfully.

He was a parasite anywhere he could worm himself into the company, maneuvering skillfully, taking advantage of any possible means to avoid an expenditure. When he ran into someone he knew in a bar or restaurant, he would see to it that his drinks and Liz's got paid for. He studied friends' habits, thus knowing to go to the Maple Hill around five on weekdays when Charlie Dunbar would be there. If he recognized a famous figure—the Cincinnati Reds' catcher Johnny Bench was one—he immediately sought a seat near him, carried on about his great career, cited statistics, and frequently was treated to drinks. Such figures are accustomed to fans' adulation but may not have good defensive instincts; Johnny Bench was, we understood, captive for a long while.

Billy Richards knew better. He recounted how he and his wife, having gone to Biloxi for a few days to get away, wanting to see no one, were accosted by Herb in a hotel eatery. Was that the occasion upon which Herb grabbed a pickle from Billy's plate, saying, just before popping it into his mouth, "Are you using that pickle?" On a similar occasion, Billy simply got up and fled as soon as Herb, espying him, turned his way. Once, Paul himself, on a stressful day, to be identified below as the *Chicago Manual of Style* day, lost his temper with Herb, who had rung at the door around 11 AM, and told him to go away.

A few scenes, reported by Herb himself or witnessed by Paul, are worth evoking in detail. One involved his brother-in-law, in Indiana, who ejected him from his house—not so much for sponging on him as for his awful social conduct. The host was married to Liz's sister. Herb and Liz had driven there, without announcing their visit, in their VW camper, which they parked in their hosts' driveway. They could sleep in it, but it had no cooking or toilet facilities; thus they were in the house most of the time. Their constant presence must have been irritating. It happened that the couple were to hold a large party one evening. The crowd included business connections. Herb got into a dispute with a man whose good will the brother-in-law did not wish to lose. The decibels rose. The phrase "threw me out" is not right, literally. Instead, the brother-in-law joined the discussion, cleverly separated Herb from his interlocutor, edged him toward the door, opened it, and pushed him out, locking it.

Another scene took place at V.L. and Nat Ewing's home. They too were to give a large party. Herb and Liz arrived without invitation but were allowed to park their van in the driveway. Nat had roasted for the buffet table a large slab of beef, then placed it in the butler's pantry to cool before transferring it to the dining table. Herb, passing through the pantry, probably in search of drink, saw the beautiful roast, opened a drawer, found a large knife, and cut from the brown, crusty top two hefty slices. Nat discovered the grievous bodily harm and identified the culprit immediately. Liz and Herb were never allowed into the house again.

On rare occasions Herb was shamed into getting out his billfold. The bishop of Alabama got five dollars from him at a church fair, pressing him to pony up as he ate and drank at bargain prices. And, I am proud to say, I got lunch for two. It was by chance that Kate and I ran into him and Liz in a Biloxi hotel, while we were there to join friends for a short spring break. It was noon. Somehow, using the fact of the surprise meeting and the hour, we managed to get invited to have lunch with them. Following his excellent example, when the bill came I did not pull out any wallet, merely thanking him for the meal.

A more impressive occasion had as its setting a Claiborne Avenue establishment called T. Pittari's, known for its shellfish and exotic meats. Three couples who had furnished food and drink to Herb and Liz many times managed to shame him into inviting them. It was agreed that Paul also must be included, having entertained him similarly. (Paul and I were not yet married.)

At T. Pittari's, Herb, ordinarily vigilant in even the smallest financial matter, let down his guard. Of course, he was not accustomed to the role of host. When cocktails were proposed and someone said "Martinis," the waiter asked, simply, "Would you like Tiger martinis?" Certainly; extra large, extra good. Next, the waiter mentioned a relish tray. The innocent host, the new Candide, again said yes. What was he thinking, that the waiter or Mr. Pittari was just a nice fellow? When the bill was brought, there was a loud scene. Since Herb never paid without going through the itemized ticket, noting the costs, contesting some (I recall an argument at the Bright Star over a nickel), subtracting the tax, sometimes drinks too, finally offering a tip of, perhaps, 10% on what remained, he saw what the Tiger martinis and relish tray had cost, and he saw the total. He exploded.

A second dinner took place at a seafood establishment called Masson's, on the lakefront. There were three couples: the reluctant host and Liz, the Ewings, and Robin Hardy with his new wife—plus Paul. Masson's was a classy place; the prices were high. Doubtless at the end of the meal Herb went through his ritual, embarrassing to others, of checking the bill meticulously. Expecting this pause, the others rose to leave. The wives went to the powder room; Paul lingered in the entryway by the coatrack; the other men left the building to bring their cars around. Suddenly two waiters burst in from the dining area, one shouting to the other, "Did you see what those bastards left me as a tip? Two dollars and a box of snuff." Then, looking around and seeing Paul, who had not managed to conceal himself completely among the coats, the man pointed and shouted, "There's one of 'em."

I cannot finish this portrait yet; I must add two touches. At a state university in Kentucky, where Herb had taken a position in the business school and bought a house, he decided that his tax bill was too high. Of course. He called on the sheriff-assessor. Now, this was a local man, in his demesne. Appalachia, if you wish, but not without lights and rights. After hearing Herb's reiterated complaints, probably peppered with allusions to his position and expertise, the fellow lost patience and, according to Herb, ordered him out of his office, calling him "an overeducated fool."

Finally, I must tell about Herb's successful application to the Harvard School of Business for an MBA in finance. It was a summer program, with sessions on campus but also an internship component at a corporation. Such arrangements provide prestige to the degree candidate, a bit of help to the corporation (one supposes), and, to

Harvard, money largely unearned. Herb was bright and perfectly able to meet the standards, as he demonstrated. But upon reading his application, an admissions officer might have questioned his motives. He was to name three cities in which he would like to be placed as a corporate intern. He wrote that he did not care as long as the city had a major league baseball team.

It is time to leave Herb and return to the years of my marriage to Paul. They were crucial to my life. The marriage kept me, I have noted, at Tulane. And those years made me a New Orleanian, a condition not envied by all, though. Who wants nearly year-round humidity, street crime, crooked politicians, dirty or broken sidewalks, streets pock-marked with potholes, giant roaches? Who wants to live in a bowl that floods? Who wants a Katrina exile? Yet I liked the city from the beginning. It became the setting for the most significant decades of my teaching and research career; it was the city of Kate's birth and remains her first home; many friendships sprang up there; and the place nourished my poetry. I liked Louisiana as a whole, also, appreciating particularly the South Louisiana culture and its bayou landscape. I came to like Thibodaux, which I visited for literary purposes.

In some ways Paul and I were a good match. I admired his moral anchor, which included a sense of duty, and his superior mind, as he applied it to scholarship in his field. But could I not have appreciated him as a colleague without marrying him? At that Chicago MLA convention, I had not paid particular attention to him. It happened, though, that in fall 1969 I was asked to drive him one evening to a restaurant, Pascal's Manale, where the French faculty would meet to entertain a visiting lecturer. I was designated to pick up Paul at a Panola Street corner two blocks from his house. My father had died shortly before. Paul spoke to me gently about the loss, with commiseration in his voice, inspired surely by remembering his own father's death.

That sympathy moved me; I was and remain easily affected by others' emotions and touched by their goodness, or appearance thereof. (I am reminded of a woman who confessed that she married her husband because on a dinner date he had offered her his asparagus.) Paul may have sensed my vulnerability, not ordinarily on display; it may have emboldened him. A sort of instinct allows men to see what usually they would not observe and simultaneously put themselves in a favorable light by taking on a character not entirely genuine, or not quotidian, at least. Mme Riccoboni, an eighteenth-century French novelist, identified in men "the art of hiding one's failings and knowing the weakness of others." Not many days after that dinner, Paul appeared at my office door, open as usual, and invited me to go with him to The Famous Door, a jazz place in the French Quarter. He would come get me in a taxi. That invitation led to further dinner dates and, not long afterwards, a proposal and marriage.[1]

Was my response thoroughly authentic (as the existentialists said)? I hope so. My sympathies are genuine, and in this case they led to romantic love. One must be wary of such feelings, though. They may conflict with other loyalties, other commitments. Gide was not wary enough; he got himself into trouble repeatedly. His comprehension was real, not superficial; he knew how others felt. But one cannot always assume others' feelings. The long, unfortunate misunderstanding between him and the poet and dramatist Paul Claudel (the brother of the sculptress Camille Claudel) is a stellar instance. Having, during difficult years (we would say he was "going through a bad time"), expressed his understanding of Claudel's sturdy Catholic faith and what it offered in the way of consolation and repose—indeed, being tempted by it—Gide then did not follow the path Claudel expected, that of conversion. Claudel lacked entirely that empathetic identification with another. He bullied Gide. The result was a lifetime quarrel.

My chief expectation in marrying Paul was that I would be a true helpmate as he pursued his scholarship and returned to a reasonably normal life. He did not particularly like teaching, but his training had prepared him for little else. And he had wanted to follow no other calling, certainly not the law, despite his father's

---

[1]   Marie-Jeanne Riccoboni, *Histoire du Marquis de Cressy* (1758).

excellent example and prominence. Oh, the prominence probably put him off—a matter not of disrespect but of temperament. Hence my husband's choice, in the absence of better, to teach. He carried out his tasks conscientiously, always. I supposed also that we would enjoy New Orleans together, have a life involving others—colleagues and friends, his mother, my family—and travel. His mother expected, she told me, that we would enlarge our horizons and he would get well away from the narrow life he had led. His mother was as mistaken as I.

Further words on his situation at Tulane are needed. He was treated somewhat like a stepchild. As his many scholarly publications warranted, he was a full professor but, a dean told him, the lowest-paid at that rank in Arts and Sciences. (Certain others, you can well imagine, published next to nothing.) True, he had no car to maintain and, in his early time there, no child to educate. But for years the medical bills and caregiver's wages had devoured his salary and more; he had been obliged to sell the wedding silver and borrow money from his mother. He was in no position to make demands. What alternative employment could he seek? At least his situation was a great improvement over that at LSUNO; he could walk to the campus, and the workload was not so heavy.

There being no single department of linguistics, he was placed in French, to handle language courses. He was sometimes lent out to Classics (for Comparative Greek and Latin Grammar) and German and Slavic Languages (for Gothic or Old High German), He was not, however, assigned classes in Old Romance tongues because two other professors, one in French, had a monopoly on the field. One simply coasted, having produced next to no research; the other, after putting out suitable work earlier, spent many hours on a slope near a women's dormitory admiring the girls who sunbathed there. After some years and a campaign I engineered, inspired by an analogous case, and with the help of a new provost, Paul was scheduled for an occasional Old French class.

Why do I include such details and many others about Paul's life—some, tempests in a teapot, you may say? For more than two decades, our lives were, legally and practically, the same. My partner was the person who had endured one hard year after another and had been changed thereby. To say he did not deserve such fate is to state the obvious; few would, and he did not bring it upon himself.

He was, perhaps, close to exhaustion. I persuaded him, at least, to eat lunch when he was at home and always prepared nutritious dinners. The lunch consisted of milk and cereal, one of three varieties among which he rotated—healthy fare, if not ideal. But his vitality, like his blood pressure, remained low. Teaching and dealing with campus duties and the inevitable clashes with others (not that he sought them—but he could not abandon his firm principles) were hard on him; he vomited every morning upon rising, before lighting his first cigarette.

He was bitter; I was not. I was forward-looking; he wanted to retreat. I put my faith and energy into that new marriage, with a baby after a year and, late that same year, a house, well located, on Willow Street, less than a mile from our building at Tulane and close to schools for our daughter. Family needs always came first, as is proper. Little children require care, and to invest time in them is good. As little children go, Kate was not much trouble, and she charmed many. Joe de Fulco, Paul's barber, called her "Bambino." An acquaintance we met at the Bright Star, from Iowa, used the term "Punkin," which I knew and liked. We had a housekeeper, the trusted Alice, who previously had tended to the bedridden wife. Five days a week, she did the housework and, during our hours on campus, kept Kate, allowing Paul and me to meet all our university obligations without begging off for childcare. But much domestic work remained for evenings and weekends. She did not cook, though she would peel shrimp and rinse lettuce for me ahead of time.

Friends of today may be astonished to know that I prepared dinner six times a week and even created special dishes on occasion—not really new, but time-consuming. Bran muffins, made from scratch, were a great hit, as was the tuna pie I devised, making the crust from scratch also. "Honey-Baked Beans," using a recipe furnished by the sister-in-law of a friend of Mother's, found favor with family and guests alike. What I call mountain-fried potatoes (prepared from leftover baked spuds) went over well. Most appreciated of all were veal croquettes, cone-shaped, which required inordinate time. When Kate was old enough to do so, she liked to help me dip the little cones into egg mixture and roll them in crumbs. As staples we had hamburgers, fried catfish, beef roast, or red beans and rice with sausage. Occasionally I cooked liver for Paul; on those evenings Kate and I ate macaroni and cheese. At Thanksgiving and Christmas I roasted a capon. For great occasions, we had *boeuf à la bourguignonne* from a French recipe. When George Dunbar gave us a quartet of wild ducks he had shot across the lake, I roasted them for a dinner party. On another occasion I gave a seated dinner for fourteen.

No more! A New Orleans friend of mine kept her best set of china in her oven. She had fed her husband and two children, seventeen years apart; then she quit cooking. Now I understand. I do not, however, buy complete dinners, nor "order in"; never in my life have I done that. I buy a few deli items and cook the rest, or use leftovers, my own, restaurant fare, or food gifts from friends. I do not use a microwave.

At the university, it was supposed that I would continue to put out scholarly work in my fields, late nineteenth- and twentieth-century French literature. I taught both advanced literature courses and those in language. With these obligations and my writing, much of the 1970s passed me by. I remember only a few dates: Watergate and Nixon's resignation (hands waving), the conclusion to the war in Vietnam (helicopters rising, desperate people), a few personal events. The latter included travel by train, with Paul, the reluctant traveler, and Kate, to Virginia in 1973 for a poetry reading; our car trip to Denver, then Alpine, in 1972; a second trip to Alpine in 1976; and my mother's death in 1979.

Paul and I were alike in our university habits. We both arrived in class on time and finished when the bell rang (yes, bells were customary then, until administrators ended the practice—too despotic?); we both returned tests at the following class; we both were no-nonsense types. An anecdote will illustrate the point. Outside his office, at the beginning of a semester, two young men, surely unwilling students in foreign language but obliged to meet the requirement, were examining the printed schedule of classes, with course title, hours, and professor's name. (Digital schedules were yet to come.) One read out to the other under the heading "French 201": "P. Brosman, 10:00; C. Brosman, 11:00. Is that the good Brosman?" The reply was succinct: "There is no good Brosman."

Paul had no objection to my academic career as such and ordinarily did not criticize it; how could he, since he had met me in a collegiate context? But the means to success (long library hours, dealings with journal editors, occasional scholarly meetings without him) and especially my poetry, to which, in time, I was able to devote more attention, must have struck him as rival concerns. And, unfortunately, I was popular—not like a professor in another department (to take one example) whose sobriquet was "Make an A with Ray," but generally liked and respected by students, colleagues, and friends in New Orleans and elsewhere. My position on his radar thus varied, according to the degree of friendliness or hostility he felt at the time and the amount of alcohol he had ingested.

He had little idea of how to establish a suitable conjugal relationship. He had been taught that he was to give presents on birthdays and at Christmas. These were obligations, learned and accepted by the autistic child, carried over into adulthood. But loving gestures should not be merely an obligation. He had no imagination for other acknowledgments of ties and affection. Thanks and compliments were rare. He reminds me of a character in a deathbed scene in Sartre's *La Nausée*. The dying man gathers around him his family and servants. Thanking all the latter for their loyal service, he turns to his wife: "You, Thérèse, I don't thank. You just did your duty."

In fact, though, I did not need compliments. What was hard to endure was Paul's hostility, the dark side. It involved a deep-set need, often frustrated, to control others, a need that arose, doubtless, from his lack of self-confidence. Psychologists have terms for such feelings of inadequacy and insecurity; no need to use them. He developed suspicions; they led to accusations. Looking through my dresser drawers, he would find suspect items, such as a silver pin with the monogram "CS," which he took to be a present from some man elsewhere. In fact, it was given to me at the end of a semester in Florida by María Elena Sánchez, a somewhat older student than most and married. (I recall that in the course she had just completed, the readings included Claudel's long poem *Magnificat*, at once a religious and a personal ode, dealing with childbirth. How apt it was: after the final examination she got on her bicycle and pedaled herself to the university hospital, where her husband would join her after work and she gave birth to their first child.) That and similar discoveries Paul made led to explosions of jealousy, groundless, that would rival Othello's, with flimsier pretexts than a handkerchief in another's possession.

Paul's mother died in 1972, leaving him her estate, which he husbanded carefully. By 1979, when we had paid off the mortgage on our house and his income from investments was steady, I persuaded him to resign from Tulane. We were accustomed to split expenses, roughly; he could pay his half. The move must have done him considerable good; the daily vomiting ceased almost immediately. He seemed generally content to spend his weekdays alone, his other hours with his wife and daughter.

Kate turned ten in 1981. My maternal duties had evolved to fit her age and the circumstances. All her schooling then was in the neighborhood, first at Newcomb Nursery School, right by our building at Tulane, then St. Andrew's Episcopal School, five blocks from our house, to which I walked with her in the mornings and a child-minder (Alice's replacement) or Paul walked for afternoon pickup duty. At what age she started going on her own I cannot say. Paul's parents were Episcopalians, and I attended Episcopal churches out of preference for the discretion with which services were conducted, the hymnology, and the aesthetics of music, architecture, and decoration.

For seventh and eighth grades, Kate attended a Presbyterian school a mile or so away; I dropped her off in the morning, and she could take the streetcar or walk home in the afternoons. Her high school, Benjamin Franklin, a public school requiring a score of 120 on an IQ test, was less than a mile in the other direction. For two years she attended concurrently NOCCA, the public creative arts school, where Ellis Marsallis taught and his sons were students. She was given a little car at age sixteen. I took time to sing in the St. Andrew's choir during four years and served as chairman of a headmaster search committee at the school.

Research and publication proceeded. In 1983 my study on Sartre appeared in the Twayne World Authors series. It was very well received, even by specialists, and for many years was the best-seller in that series, going into paperback. (To be sure, that success derived from his fame, not mine.) In addition, as the 1980s drew to a close, I had to my credit a short book on the writer-aviator Jules Roy, a full-length study on him, and, as editor and contributor, three hefty volumes on the twentieth-century French novel in the Dictionary of Literary Biography series. Those publications led to a faculty Research Prize.

Paul pursued his scholarship and published many articles. He had his own working library to support his research; I checked out from the Tulane library additional books. When editors of learned journals proved prickly to work with, I encouraged him not to throw away his manuscripts, but, rather, find another home for them. I typed his letters and occasionally whole papers; or I delivered them to a typist or mailed them to someone across Lake Pontchartrain. Once in a while, we attended an academic meeting at which he spoke, wanting to present publicly certain results of his work. I recall typing the final pages of a paper on the evening before we were to take the train to Atlanta.

Yet all was not smooth, though I strove mightily, for everyone's sake, to have harmony at home and keep the marriage going. I called on self-discipline, efficiency, and moral effort. I remember the comment of a professor from an Ivy League campus when I said that I could not attend an upcoming conference because my husband wanted me at home. "But with all your intelligence ...? And you seem so independent." "Thanks for your confidence in me," I replied; "but I put that intelligence into preserving my marriage."

I suppose that Paul felt unappreciated, unloved, perhaps. Oh, dear; the thought is not good. An only child, he had to share me with many others, to whom, necessarily and often willingly, I paid attention. Blame goes probably to his autism, which I have stressed; it kept his world narrow and his views inflexible. Insecurity, I have written. What he felt may resemble the pain Andre Dubus III ascribes to himself: "the superior pain of the inferior, the pride of the sufferer." And Paul, passive by nature, had, by retiring, put himself into a position of dependency and vulnerability—the one acted on, not acting.

A Houston friend of mine recounted to me how one evening her husband and she entered a doughnut shop, near closing time. She made her choice right away and said so to the server, a young woman, who looked very tired. The husband hesitated, studying the offerings, changing his mind. My friend urged him to make his selection so that they could leave and the server could close the shop. "You love her more than you love me!" was his response. (That was my friend's first marriage. The marriage was dissolved. It is pleasing to add that her second marriage was a good one.)

Two incidents from my experience may be cited. One is connected to my affection for Evelyn Payne. Paul was vexed to learn that a book of mine about to appear bore a dedication to her. Like the doughnut shop employee, she was not in the family, but in my eyes, she deserved special courtesy. (He got a dedication later.) When my copies came and he looked at one, he asked, "What has she done for you?" Well, she was my friend, a lifetime friend. Her interest in literature paralleled mine; she displayed my books and recent journal publications on an angled shelf in a living room bookcase.

The second incident, from fifteen years later, is connected to Paul's book *The Rhine Franconian Element in Old French* (1999). Although typists had prepared most of the original files, I assembled them, created the front matter, made changes he wanted in the content, typed new material, then created and typed the index. I typed the multiple letters that led, finally, to his securing a publisher. Following the publisher's strict demands, I put everything into double-column camera-ready copy. No small job. Yet one morning he became annoyed because I asked whether he had my copy of *The Chicago Manual of Style*, left with him for consultation on form but needed then by me. He snapped. Having gone upstairs to get it, he hurled it down the staircase at me, shouting. That was the day on which he told Herb and Liz, who appeared at the front door without warning, to leave and cease bothering him. You notice that neither here nor elsewhere do I mention any words of apology. Once, after a similar scene but worse, (like many), he did offer to take me to *Don Giovanni*, to be presented at Tulane. That was extraordinary.

He and I had been divorced for six years. It is painful to write that fear for my own safety and Kate's had led me to take the drastic step of leaving the household. With her maturing, it had become possible for me to undertake more scholarship, more writing than before, and I wanted to go (and went) to Europe for research and traveled around the U.S. to literary and scholarly conferences. Such travel did not sit well with Paul; he felt his control waning. He had not raised a hand against me, but increasingly he displayed terrific anger, brought about by his delusions. (Neighbors separated from us by only a narrow driveway, thus within easy earshot, told me later that they had wondered how I could endure it all.) I came to fear that his rage might prove uncontrollable and lead to violence. Kate had similarly gained independence. When I left, she was at the University of Chicago for her last year, thus safely away from the scene of the drama, though she had witnessed a good deal previously. Some months later, divorce clarified the domestic situation and made possible subsequent accommodations in Paul's favor, about which you will read.

His friend Herb later remarked that my leaving must have been prompted by Paul's cigars, which had replaced cigarettes. Certainly not! They were incidental; I can accommodate much. Indeed, I put up with his smoking one thing or another for more than two decades and for years afterwards, when we reached a modus vivendi, though divorced and living apart.

I wept upon leaving the neighborhood of the Willow Street house. My attempts to preserve an increasingly shaky marriage had ended in failure. What I could hope for was safety and—though they were not yet visualized—some elements of the relationship preserved as new successes.

These pages are not intended principally as an indictment, and I regret having to evoke such conduct. I would not do so if the trajectory, or plot, of this story did not call for it. That is, since I ultimately left the household, I must show why. Paul meant a great deal to me. I keep on my desk an old legal pad marked "U-stems," the short title of an article of his.

Catharine in Her Garden District Condominium.
Photograph by Thomas Vincent Van Auken, Jr.

Chapter Ten

The Garden District

The Garden District is a jewel neighborhood of New Orleans, a city of distinct districts, each with its own attributes: the French Quarter, the Marigny, the Bywater, the Tremé, Gentilly, the Lower Garden District, Carrollton, Mid-City, City Park, Bayou St. John, and still others. The Garden District is known for its beautiful nineteenth-century Greek Revival cottages and mansions, as well as small shotguns, almost all beautifully painted in white or pastel colors.

I lived there for more than fifteen years, not in a fine cottage or small house, but a condominium apartment building at St. Charles Avenue and Second St. It was built in 1963, before the district had been put on the National Register of Historic Places. Even with the historic designation, more than one new building has since been erected in the immediate environs. Called the Andrew Jackson, the building to which I moved, of gray-green stucco, had no southern character, except for the surnames of numerous residents from old New Orleans families. The style was, roughly, East German. Fortunately, it was solid.

I first leased a one-bedroom unit from Karlheinz and Ingrid Hasselbach. The Hasselbachs had come to the States separately, each with a German Ph.D.; Karlheinz had an excellent command of English. They met and married in Florida, then moved when

Karlheinz was appointed to Tulane. As Germans who knew earlier twentieth-century history and were old enough to have lived through World War II and its horrible aftermath, they had little trust in currency and banks; thus they invested their savings in real estate, owning three or four properties, two divided into rentals. We were good friends; we sometimes attended the symphony concerts together. Their little place in the Andrew Jackson did nicely for me.

When a larger unit just across the hall was up for sale, I bought it. It was well designed for parties, a mid-sized bedroom adjoining the main room having been transformed into a study and piano room, with bookshelves and wide doorways. I added a pull-out love seat. Overnight guests, some from Europe, could occupy the bedroom, while I slept in the study. Numerous parties, some quite large, remain in my memory. Gay Smith, the wife of a graduate student and a skilled hostess and cook, helped me give two dinners for twelve. And I often entertained a small cluster of neighbors, including Elizabeth Beelman, the mother of my friend Michèle's husband; two lamps of hers now illuminate my New Orleans pied-à-terre, acquired recently.

Kate returned from Chicago, exceptionally, for Thanksgiving in the autumn of 1992, and then again at Christmas and in the spring, between quarters. Until she spent a year in Paris (1996-1997) and then married, that pattern held. She stayed with her father, but from the beginning the three of us met for afternoons and evenings. The hours together brought Paul and me closer, as did the numerous occasions on which I picked him up to take him to appointments. By 1993 I had reestablished, carefully, a pattern of social contacts for us. I suggested resuming our custom of going regularly on Friday evenings to the Bright Star. I would drive to Willow Street, then drop him off at the end of the evening. After he had words with the management, we started going up South Carrollton Avenue to Ye Olde College Inn. We deserted that establishment in turn, however, and began frequenting the Rendon Inn, in the Broadmoor neighborhood, quite some distance.

I also traveled frequently, first to West Texas, in May. I was eager to get away—not *from*, but *to*. If, as Sartre insisted, one is different among others, and variably so, according to the company, then it's plausible to think that one responds variously according to locations also. "You seem so different here," said Jack Miller (one of cousin Jean's sons) and his wife, Jeannie, as we drove together one September through South Louisiana and the approaches to its great city. Travel remains for me an old habit, maybe juvenile. We are told that one should put away "childish things" but not that child-like spirit which enables us to take joy in little moments and small pleasures, greeting each day with anticipation.

In the winter of 1993, when I was on leave in order to work on *French Culture 1900-1975*, I went to New Jersey for a short appointment as a Fellow at Rutgers University. There I presented aspects of my research on war literature in France and conferred with scholars having similar interests. Later that semester I traveled to Philadelphia to present at a conference a different paper, on war iconography. In 1994 I flew to England, then crossed to the continent. On the occasion of another visit to England in May 1995, I was invited to stop at universities in Keele, Lancaster, and Sheffield,

The following year, I had the opportunity to spend the winter and spring terms as De Velling and Willis Visiting Research Professor at Sheffield. The title and appointment belonged, as I understood it, to the university as a whole, to be assigned by rotation or need. French got it that year. My duties were few. Chiefly, I contributed my publication list to the Department of French to swell its credentials for review by an outside commission, on the results of which would depend its reputation and increased funding. I gave a lecture to a university-wide audience as well as talks to the department. Each month I went to London to work at the old British Library, still located then in Bloomsbury (my preferred London neighborhood), and I addressed groups at two colleges there. The London theatres did well by me, over and over. Scholars at Norfolk and Essex saw to it that an invitation to speak came my way.

That winter, 1996, the weather was beastly in the Midlands, and the spring barely existed. But the people I came to know in the French department at Sheffield and elsewhere were warm and generous. A Londoner, retired from Glasgow, whose name I did not know, telephoned me in Sheffield to welcome me to England; subsequently, we met in London often and enjoyed gallery visits together. A retired couple right in Sheffield sent a car through the snow to fetch me for dinner at their house. The former head of department held a large dinner party in my honor. Annie Rouxéville and her husband, John Peak, invited me often and took me around to villages and historical or architectural sites. David Walker, then head of department, and his wife, Lesley, were similarly welcoming, organizing dinners and including me in family expeditions. I revisited Lancaster and lectured at Leicester, welcomed by Peter and Margot Fawcett, who became firm friends. In London, Patrick Pollard invited me to the flat he shared with his bookseller friend. The charm, wit, and generosity of all these Brits, most of whom I saw during subsequent visits, are memorable.

I crossed the Channel to Paris in May 1996 on one of the initial runs of the Eurostar. June was given partly to travel in Central Europe (Berlin, Prague, and Budapest). July was dedicated wholly to teaching in a Tulane program housed in a former monastery in Normandy, near Caen. The program director and fellow faculty member was my friend David Clinton, in Political Science. After a return to Sheffield for most of August, I attended a Gide symposium in the Cotentin (Normandy) and, finally, flew back to New Orleans for my final semester at Tulane. Readers can identify in numerous poems and *Finding Higher Ground: A Life of Travels* reflections of that period.

Retirement came at the beginning of 1997 when I accepted a "golden handshake," with parachute. My agenda was full, and varied. That winter LSU Press accepted my book *Fiction, Art, Ideology: Images of War in France* (1999). I was at work on poems, which became *Places in Mind* (2000), and on personal essays, which furnished much material for *Finding Higher Ground*.

I produced translations of Pernette du Guillet for a series that did not, unfortunately, materialize; some found their way into one of my poetry collections. At the end of the decade I composed *The Swimmer and Other Poems* and two companion books, one on Camus, the other on existential fiction, chiefly in French. Those studies and the volume on war literature are among my best scholarly work.

As the century ended, in addition to visits in Houston and Austin, to see friends, and Colorado Springs, I had three larks—no, I'll call them junkets, "investigations" as well as R&R, but paid for by me, of course. I went twice to the US Virgin Islands, once to St. Croix, a bit later to St. Thomas. Those week-long stays offered unusually lovely vegetation and also social pleasures. Reflections of the two visits are found in *The Muscled Truce*. The third junket was to Aspen, in late winter, when two casual friends pressed me to go and attend the famous "Sneaker Ball," written up in *Finding Higher Ground*.

Enough for the moment, or too much! It is time to say more about the accommodation between Paul and me, a bizarre one, but the best I could do. A new custom arose to bolster the Friday get-togethers. On Sunday evenings, I packed in a Red-Riding-Hood basket a casserole, took it to Willow Street, heated and served it, and stayed for the evening; or I'd cook something for us there taken over from my own pantry or groceries that I delivered to him then or earlier in the week. We'd watch the news or, in season, the late football games.

Except during my frequent absences, we followed this routine, and I also saw Paul during the week when I delivered books or his grocery order. I took him to his doctor's, near Touro Infirmary, and an eye practice in Metairie, even a dentist's across the lake. On a longer venture, we drove with his cat and mine, Dill, a waif I'd taken in, to the Florida Panhandle during a spring vacation to join Kate, Brian, the first baby, Clara, and Brian's parents at a modest resort. Paul did not do well but survived, at least.

After the turn of the century, finding the evening driving tedious and concerned about his safety—a man past seventy by himself in a two-story house, with few lights on and no car in the garage—I proposed that he purchase a little condo in my Garden District building. Initially he did not agree. I then thought of a way to brighten his life, a surprising but workable plan. I would take him, the one who did not like travel, to southern Illinois by car, to visit his father's town, Albion. He agreed. He had not seen it, I believe, since America became involved in World War II. Leaving his dog and the two cats with a sitter, we set out on I-55 north. We stopped one night at a hotel in Grenada, Mississippi ("This is my bed; that is your bed"—the same arrangement we had when we attended Kate's graduation from Chicago in 1993).

Albion is a very small town. We stayed In Mount Vernon, at a good Holiday Inn at which I had booked a suite, with a separate bedroom and bath for Paul and a pull-out bed in the main room for me. He paid extra in order to be able to smoke his cigars. We spent most of one day in Albion and its immediate environs. I recall the town square, but apart from it there was little to see. Still, he was glad to have been there. We stayed a few more days, watching both football and baseball (the World Series). We had to cheer for the St. Louis Rams, given that we went to the bar every evening, where no other fan would be safe. Southern Illinois is a long way from Chicago.

On the return trip, I chose a different route. Somewhere in Tennessee, in the midst of spaghetti freeways and orange-cone configurations, I got lost. Squeezed into a single-lane portion, I saw that we were headed directly to Nashville. Now, such surprises do not bother me much. One drives ahead until it's possible to turn around or turn off. Paul was distressed; he liked no surprises. My serenity amazed him and may have helped him. Surely that little road venture did, for the next time I inquired about his moving to a smaller place, knowing that a condo was for sale on my very floor of the Andrew Jackson, he agreed. Kate and Brian flew down in June to help him ready the house for sale and move his furniture and books into his new abode.

He came to feel at home there. We maintained a very agreeable routine. Friday evenings out (he paid); dinners provided by me on Sundays; his groceries delivered when I got mine; and even a mini-martini for me at 5:30 each evening in his condo, where we watched the news. I started inviting him to bring his cereal box and milk jug to eat lunch with me if I was at home.

Most days were peaceable. One morning, when I informed him that the next day I would drive to Thibodaux to participate in a literary festival, he was seized by wrath and shouted at me. Should I have foreseen such an episode? Perhaps. I had wanted to finish that afternoon a poem to be read at a workshop the following day. In my disordered state of mind, how could I do so? Somehow, it came together. I slept very little that night, however, as if to invite the accomplishment of his angry threat: "Someday you'll die on the highway driving down there." The poem, "Indian Paintbrush," is considered beautiful; it gives one a shiver.

In 2005, the exceptional circumstances of Hurricane Katrina occasioned an unusual departure, as we left some thirty-six hours after the worst of the storm, taking a cat for each of us. (The dog had died before his move.) The experience of driving from the nearly deserted city over the twin bridges to the West Bank and the sequel to that departure, a long exile, were terrible. I had had little sleep during the two nights preceding our departure—that of the storm itself and the next one—in the miasma of wet carpet and puddles from rain forced through windows and under doors and, without electricity, only cold foods, while a fine roast began to rot in the refrigerator.

It was Paul who suggested that we leave. Desperate measures for desperate men. On St. Charles at Second Street, the water did not rise so high as elsewhere generally. It had not reached my Jeep. Earlier, as the storm threatened the city, I realized, of course, that there might be flooding; but, like so many, I had lived before through hurricanes and tropical storms. Paul recalled several severe storms. Electricity would, in due course, be restored, one assumed; I would order new carpet; life would begin again. That was our first response. It happened though, by chance, that Paul had a small pocket-sized radio that an acquaintance had given him. He had never touched it. He remembered it, turned it on, and learned from the one radio station on the air, WWL, broadcasting feebly from some West Bank location, that on Canal Street 11 ½ inches of water were flowing. That fact changed the whole picture: it could no longer be accumulated rain; it was a surge from the lake through broken floodgates.

He appeared at my door, reported what he had heard, and asked, "Should we leave?" "Of course—if it is possible." In thirty-five minutes we were gone, each with a cat in its carrier, each with a small suitcase packed in great haste. We had money, he in cash, I with credit cards. As many readers will remember, there was only one way out, the bridge to the West Bank, all other routes being flooded or half-destroyed. We drove in a downtown direction toward the bridge approach. No traffic at all. When we encountered a full-sized oak tree lying across the downtown lanes, I crossed the neutral ground and continued on the uptown side. Again, empty. We were able to reach the Baronne Street access ramp, turn onto the bridge to the West Bank, and get across.

The route to Texas from New Orleans on old US 90 has a great loop in it, going to Morgan City, where it crosses the Atchafalaya. The highways were open. My gasoline level was a bit low, but gasoline pumps were working in Morgan City. In Lafayette, we stopped at a Wal-Mart to buy pet supplies we had forgotten. Finding along our route no motels with vacancies, I supposed we would need to drive as far as Houston for the night. But, providentially, we nabbed the last room at a large Best Western in Lake Charles. Each of us claimed a bed, and each cat got on its owner's bed, understanding, apparently, that it was no time to experiment with any other arrangement. The next day we drove to Austin.

Our hostess was Patricia Teed, who had assured me more than once in the past that I was to consider her house my hurricane refuge. We were offered two other refuges, one, a modern, fully-equipped garage apartment in Houston, on the property of my friends Mary Santina and Peter Andronaco, the other, offered by Tom and Nancy Eubank, their ranch. Though very grateful, we remained where we first landed. The city was uncongenial to me, despite Patricia's graciousness and generosity. The exile lasted more than five weeks.

What was New Orleans like, we wondered? Television allowed us to see the ruins and the mayhem, including a big bonfire on St. Charles at Third Street, right by our building. True, we were ourselves safe and dry, on a sort of barge or raft ("Le Radeau de la Méduse"); but we saw our city drowning.

Two series of my poems that reflect the experience are faithful to the spirit of the moment and details. At Patricia's house, we had good quarters—Paul, a front bedroom with a large closet and bath, I, the guest suite. with a sitting room and spacious personal quarters. Each cat stayed with its owner at night. In the daytime I opened the sitting room so we could share it. I tried to assist Patricia, whose responsibilities on the University of Texas campus, always heavy, were particularly burdensome right then. I got groceries, kept things neat in the kitchen, started dinner preparations in the late afternoon, and sometimes cooked. But, like all adults who live alone, she had very fixed habits, and my measures did not always fit well into hers.

As for Paul, the man who did not like change, he found that much was changed! Neither of us slept well on any night, or enough. The poor man was unable to concentrate on anything. He could not utilize the books I got for him from the university library, thanks to the gracious reception given me there as a Katrina refugee from the Tulane faculty. News on television, repeated hour after hour when our hostess was present, was like water-drop torture. I managed to make progress on a paper I was to deliver in London in mid-October; but it was slow-going. A burden was added by my worry over friends (Olivia Pass, formerly living in Biloxi one block from the beach waters—possibly dead; David Clinton, last seen by me on the Saturday before the storm; former and present neighbors; students dear to me, and a newly-arrived French-speaking law student from Switzerland without another contact in America).

Routines at the Austin house—two of us in the daytime, three in the evenings—were generally well-oiled. Existence was complicated when, not long after Katrina, Hurricane Rita arrived in southwest Louisiana and southeast Texas: Patricia's future daughter-in-law arrived from north Houston with her dogs, adding to the menagerie and making meals difficult, since she was a vegetarian and, moreover, lived on a student's rhythm, eating and sleeping at no fixed hours. Patricia saw to it, somehow, that we all were cared for.

Paul lost his temper and yelled at me once; too many calls on my cell phone from or about my friends were hard to bear for someone who could not take disruption easily. On our return trip to New Orleans (decided upon only when we learned that electricity had been restored and that a supermarket had reopened, with basic foodstuffs), I myself precipitated his impatience, which turned to anger. The incident took place in Louisiana, near Baton Rouge. It turned on my wanting to purchase, at a Shell convenience store and station, a hamburger to eat in the car as I resumed driving (quite feasible). It meant further delay. He was too close to home to endure it with equanimity.

Upon returning, we saw how fortunate we were. From various sources we learned who among our acquaintances had been obliged to sleep on concrete floors in Lafayette (my friends the Hasselbachs); who had been confined in the Superdome for days (Adrian, a woman staff member at the Andrew Jackson, of whom I was fond); who had lost his house (my student of yore, Frank Anselmo); who had died in the exodus (two retired professors we knew). We saw that our condo building was not in ruins, that our units, apart from my damp carpets and ruined refrigerator, had not been greatly affected. My repair costs, all out-of-pocket, to carpet, windows, and glass doors were only $25,000. I discarded a piece of furniture; the veneer having separated. That sum does not include restoration of my piano. Pianos suffer when surrounded by moisture for five weeks.

Katrina was awful and not to be risked again.

My thought was to purchase a condo or town house across Lake Pontchartrain, not right on the shore (though it would not get lake flooding) but some distance from it, in Madisonville or Hammond, a college town. I would furnish it simply, take ample books, and spend the hurricane season there, inviting Paul to come too, with a second bedroom and bathroom for him. In spring 2006, telling him why I was going, I drove across the lake and visited various properties.

Alas, there was nothing quite right for me. A town house I could have purchased that very day was located in what amounted to "Students' Row," with cars scattered about and signs of late parties. Oh, no.

The next thought was to buy a condo apartment in a high-rise in downtown Austin, within walking distance of the University of Texas Library. With that marvelous facility within a few blocks, I could have been quite satisfied and could have kept Paul as contented as possible. The prices were, you can imagine, much higher than in Hammond, but I could have afforded something suitable, thanks to investments I could sell and the generosity of my deceased friend Evelyn, who at her death left me a nice chunk of cash.

I broached the plan to Paul. "You can carry on your research with ease," I observed. But he simply could not consider leaving New Orleans, despite the sufferings that Katrina had inflicted on him. Poor man, much more neurotic than I. Or perhaps it was because, already greatly dependent on me, he could not tolerate the prospect of living for some months each year in a place I owned in what was in some ways a foreign city, without any of his New Orleans habits and friends. "In that case," I said to myself, "Colorado it will be." No hurricanes, though fire and tornadoes are summer hazards. Paul, having no taste for mountains and, clearly, unwilling to spend weeks away from New Orleans, would not entertain the thought. He was no longer to be taken into consideration. Thus I acquired my little condo in Colorado Springs, with its broad balcony and fine view of Pike's Peak. I started spending more than three months there each year.

He resented my summers away, however. No Friday nights at Frankie and Johnny's (it had replaced the Rendon Inn in his affections); no Sunday dinners. He was reduced to buying his food at a Palestinian grocery on Prytania Street, to which he could walk. At least I got for him a wheeled cart and helped him apply for a Visa card. He had never had a credit card, and the bank, in a display of idiocy, expressed reluctance to grant him one. I managed to persuade an employee to issue a card with a low but adequate limit. (Once Aunt Flora got a similar response from American Express. Having been invited by that business to apply for a card, she was then turned down because she had no credit record! She had paid for everything by cash or check.)

Nevertheless, the other months of the year were an approximate success in peaceable domestic arrangements without marriage—a truce, if you will. It was unfortunate for Paul that it ended upon my re-meeting and remarriage with Patric Savage, a story to be told in a following chapter. Why is happiness, even when it is legitimate, so often predicated upon others' misery? Why does duty frequently go against their comfort or require their sacrifice? One right cancels or competes against another right. I regretted leaving that unfortunate man, so dependent upon me.

Paul understood better then that Kate loved him and, left by himself, appreciated her devotion. It was she who gave him comfort in his illness (his only one, but fatal), flying down to see him after doctors discovered his stage-4 cancer; it was she who did the rest, getting him, as the cancer did not yield to treatment, into a hospice. He died two days after that move. It was she who arranged for a proper Christian service and placement of his ashes.

Chapter Eleven

The Poet Herself

A n eminent critic and poet, introducing me to an audience, noted the hiatus of eighteen years between my first and second collections, singling it out as surprising. He likewise has a spouse, a university position, and offspring—more children than I. But he is a man.

I recall that not in resentment nor to grouse but to underline how poems, like everything else, are produced, ultimately, in *time*— time to think, then to act (write), then to follow up on the act (send off work for publication, correspond with editors about it, collect it into a book, proofread, and other tasks). *Ars longa, vita brevis.* Nevertheless, I managed, with perseverance and sacrifice of other pleasures, to write my poems and publish them.

One does not live nor write in solitude, nor publish alone. My literary debts are enormous, to press directors, publicists, acquisition staff, and journal editors, among them the late George Core, who accepted my first collection for the University of Georgia Press and subsequently, as editor of the *Sewanee Review*, published scores of my poems along with prose. Others to be mentioned are Charles East and John Easterly of LSU Press, Marc Jolley of Mercer University Press, and Clyde N. Wilson, of Shotwell Publishing. Lewis P. Simpson and Donald Stanford, both deceased, took poems time and time again for the *Southern Review*. I am indebted likewise

Catharine reading from her poetry,
Lafayette, Louisiana, May 2024
Photograph by Melissa Bonin

to reviewers and endorsers of my books, as well as friends and unknowns who lent their personalities and stories to my verse. Nor should I forget those friends who have bought copies of my books over and over and helped organize readings and book tours—Olivia Pass and Richard Cranford, among them.

In discussions after readings, people inquire about the origins of my poetry and its background. "When did you start writing?" "Why do you write?" "What inspires you?" "What poets have influenced you?" or "Who are your favorites?" "Did you take creative writing classes?" These questions make sense; they acknowledge a vague understanding that poetry is far above any ordinary leisure activity; indeed, it is among the highest expressions of human understanding. (Questions such as "Do you write at the same time every day?" or "Do you always sit at a desk?" are not worth answering.)

I was born a poet, or so I have written. Does the statement make any sense? Or, maybe, I was born a versifier but made myself into a poet. As a very small child, I heard verse quoted and sung and responded to it. My parents read aloud to me from anthologies for children, including R.L. Stevenson's famous collection. My mother appreciated hymns from the English Wesleyan and nineteenth-century American traditions and was thus familiar with rhyme and meter and understood metaphors, many drawn from the Bible itself, such as *rock* and *light*. My father passed on to me his love of the British poetic tradition. With better health than his, longer life, perhaps other gifts, I have been able to realize a poet's vocation. I have put into words sometimes what may have been his thoughts

Such an enterprise is, as I have argued in essays, not frivolous, not simply an entertainment or a self-indulgent expression. As William Hazlitt put it, "Poetry is the universal language the heart holds with nature itself.... It is not a mere frivolous accomplishment of a few idle readers and leisure hours—it has been the study of mankind in all ages." Like all the fine arts when practiced well, poetry contributes to refinement of life. It is among those enterprises which examine and preserve the past, while sifting and shaping it to increase understanding, appreciation, and judgment, so that human beings may know themselves and comprehend their destiny better.[1]

A reader or listener does not have to notice what is going on; it can happen simply through the language (the key to our mind). Poetry appeals, thus, to some who have not expected to be affected. At readings, audience members may say, afterwards, how they had not supposed they would like the presentation—they came through social duty or on professorial command—but were amazed to find the poems appealing. A reading at Macon State University once drew a large audience, filling an amphitheatre. It was composed mostly, I'm confident, of undergraduates whose instructors had sent them with the promise of points on the next test or a similar reward. They found the poems entertaining and meaningful. I recall how they applauded vigorously and laughed at "Portobello Mushrooms."

Just today I received a moving message from Michèle Beelman expressing her gratitude to me, alluding subtly to her dissertation topic (Valéry) but highlighting more my own poems, some of which she and her late husband admired particularly. (One is dedicated to them.) She was surprised to find that he, chiefly a businessman, liked to read from my collections at night in bed! I did not achieve this by myself; some spirit working in me led to the vision, then the words, which are *one*.

Which leads me to quote Proust: "Style is a matter not of technique but of vision." What is popularly called *inspiration* is that vision, at a nebulous stage, perhaps. Ipso facto, the vision is ultimately the poetry itself. It is not a thesis nor a statement. The nineteenth-century poet Mallarmé, a model for numerous admirers, observed to his famous painter friend, Edgar Degas, who said he could not manage to put his ideas into poetic form, "My dear Degas, poetry does not consist of ideas. but of words." The rational Valéry, while conceding that behind the poem lay something that one can call "thought," argued that still farther back, at its origin, more subtly, lay something else, a pre-thought, maybe a rhythm, a feeling. Shakespeare spoke

---

[1] Hazlitt, "On Poetry in General," 1818.

of poetry as "a fine frenzy." That's not an idea. Consider others' poems you may remember. If you reduce them to newspaper prose you destroy them. Gide wrote that poetry was "the gift of being moved by plums" (that is, by little nothings). You may recall the delightful lines on that topic, beginning "This is just to say," by William Carlos Williams; you may know my short lyric "Plums."[2]

Broadly speaking, my poems fall into three formal categories: traditional lines, rhymed and in meter; blank verse (usually iambic pentameter without rhyme); and free verse, but quite chastened, usually structured in stanzas of four or eight lines, with beat. I am thus almost a "formal poet." But I am not one of the New Formalists, connected to the West Chester Poetry Conference; I belong to no school. My diction and syntax are entirely contemporary; I eschew anything that sounds like Tennyson or the Georgian poets, particularly inversions that are now out of date. Poems can be roughly classed also by mood and content: for instance, lyrical, meditative, narrative, and philosophical—my work illustrates all these loose types—as well as dramatic, hortative, epic, oratorical, and others.

My writing, or "inspiration," was not without connection to teaching; both endeavors employ and illustrate language and its possibilities. My skills were advanced particularly during many classes touching on French poetry of the late nineteenth and twentieth centuries, whether in introductory doses to students in the skill-level classes or in large chunks to upper-level and graduate students. Despite significant differences between French and English prosody, the prolonged acquaintance with major figures of the period, the repeated exposure to recognized masterpieces and honored short lyrics, and the responses of students offered training.

Among poets I have in mind are Baudelaire, for what Victor Hugo termed "un frisson nouveau" (a new shiver); Verlaine, for lyrics to memorize; Rimbaud, for his utter individualism and his lightning-like strikes of illumination; and the great modernist Guillaume Apollinaire, for free verse, especially what he called the *poème-conversation*. The name of the perfectionist Valéry recurs in

---

[2]   In *Range of Light*.

these pages for good reason. A model of taste, discipline, and style in formal verse, he understood, as so many do not, that sheer feeling does not suffice to make a poem. "To feel does not mean to make felt; still less, *beautifully felt*." I think also of St-John Perse, René Char, and Claudel, an unpleasant, overbearing man, full of himself, hypocritical to boot, but whose great *Odes* are marvelous. Gide, a major prose stylist, whom I just cited, remains in my pantheon for his insistence on aesthetic values. Occasionally in my poems one finds an exclamatory "Ah!" of the sort he used.

The great body of lyric, satiric, devotional, and dramatic poetry in England is, of course, the foundation of all my verse. The point is obvious. The English iambic pentameter is in my head, always. Its brilliant illustrations by Shakespeare and his contemporaries and close followers remain models to this day. Notwithstanding the appeal of other rhythms, it leads the parade. While over the past hundred years innumerable poets have tried to get away from it, the results are frequently less than pleasing. It appears widely in today's free verse, even when unsought, and is fundamental in mine, contributing to its classic discipline. As for lines that have no rhythm at all, they will always sound like prose ("Without rhythm, the poem is dead," wrote Don Stanford.)

Those wanting me to name my favorite poets are often disappointed when I reply, since they mean not canonic figures from British and American literature but recent writers, names in the literary news. First, I mention Americans they should know from school: Poe and Dickinson. Next comes the Nobel laureate Eliot, though his reputation has fallen recently because critics have identified in his writing Gentile racism. I have in mind his later verse, though I appreciate the irony of the early poems. More recent figures who can be mentioned, just to give a few *points de repère*, are James Dickey, Richard Wilbur, and Dana Gioia. Readers of my two historical studies on poets of Louisiana and Mississippi know that I am an admirer of certain poets of recent decades in those states.

As for my personal literary connections, they have been cir-
cumspect and circumscribed, partly by facts of geography and sex,
more by my own preferences. As Claude Wilkinson noted in a book
endorsement, I have not paid court to taste-makers and others of
influence, nor compromised my aesthetic ideals. At no time did I
wish to give up a stable, and rewarding, university life to try my luck
as a free-lancer, journalist, or gofer in publishing in New York or
San Francisco. (I don't want to live in a garret. Today I could not
live even there without private income or a job.) In the introduction
to this book, I noted the middle-class figures Robert Frost, Wallace
Stevens, and William Carlos Williams. I have known a small number
of impressive contemporaries, including those poets with whom I
became acquainted in Virginia. I must mention also the late John
William Corrington, of Louisiana. I correspond with other poets of
today, among them the California figure Constance Rowell Mastores.

What about France? I had the privilege of being well acquainted
with outstanding figures: Jules Roy—novelist, essayist, poet,
dramatist; the poet Jean-Claude Renard; and the novelist and critic
Bertrand Poirot-Delpech, who entered the Académie.

On the subject of creative writing courses in poetry, I have gone
on record before to say that they are often of dubious value and
should generally be avoided. Donald Hall is among the contemporary
writers who have expressed the same view. David R. Slavitt refers to
"Gradgrind workshops." Those who teach them are mostly people
"who have no apparent talent for [poetry]—or even interest in it—
but have taken it up because it is indoor work that doesn't involve
heavy lifting." At Rice there was no course on poetic practice. I did,
however, take two classes dealing with fiction-writing, taught by a
learned faculty member, George G. Williams, who had published a
novel of note. His approach was double. We read others' fiction and
essays on the art, and we wrote our own stories and undertook a
novel project. His reading selections were judicious, and I learned
thereby a great deal about literature. The only discussions on poetry
took place in a club he sponsored that met at his house.

A word is needed concerning my extensive output—fifteen collections now, with two more planned, and hundreds of poems published individually in journals, magazines, and anthologies, many translated into French (by others). Such extensive output cannot be uniformly excellent. The collected poems of Ted Hughes, once Poet Laureate of England, constitute a very thick tome; no one could make the case that they are all superior. Rather, in his case, as in mine, the numbers illustrate breadth and variety. Within that range are, presumably, examples of the author's best craftmanship and finest sensibilities. Moreover, there is strength in numbers, that is, recurrent treatments of topics that lend themselves to varied lighting and angles. As Monet said about his series of paintings showing haystacks, Rouen cathedral, and London, the full value of the works may lie in the repetition and the comparisons it offers.

In 1996, David Slavitt, whom I quoted just above, wrote in connection with my volume *Passages*, "Why she hasn't been laden with honors and awards is an unfathomable mystery to me." Readers may think of good reasons not to give me any. Someone else may need them more than I. Reviewers, whom I've mentioned as deserving my gratitude, have given me very good press, over and over, in respected publications; those assessments and the poems themselves hold up. To add that I am not the prize-winning type is a question, not an answer. Prizes, be it known, even Pulitzers, are not all they are cracked up to be. As Joseph Epstein said of major literary awards, with very little exaggeration, "Everyone gets a trophy, and no trophy is worth anything."[3]

This moment is appropriate for tracing broadly the themes in my work, as I see them. (Others may see better, though.) Such considerations are suited to this enterprise of memoirs, woman and work being closely connected. Much thematic material is derived from my travels and others', while a major vein is travel itself, the

---

[3]   See Slavitt, "The Year in Poetry," *Dictionary of Literary Biography Yearbook*, 1996, pp. 11, 26, and my piece on Donald Hall in *Chronicles: A Magazine of American Culture*, October 2018. https://chroniclesmagazine.org/editorials-what-good-poetry-can-be/ See also the poem "Dickey at Rice" (*On the North Slope*). The Epstein quotation comes from the *Wall Street Journal*, 18-19 May 2024.

experience of displacement, motion, and being thus, temporarily, *other*. Teaching a class on poetry once at Nicholls State in Thibodaux as a guest, and having read and commented on some of my poems to illustrate my points, I was asked by a student what one was to do when travel was impossible. The unfortunate young man was crippled, in a wheelchair. His point was well taken. Someone without any financial resources might ask the same question; there are many such along the bayous of South Louisiana and everywhere. Clearly, the answer was to read, to study photographs and films, in the public libraries if one cannot get one's own copies. Those are the means we all use to understand that which none of us can visit—the past.

Nature—mountains, desert, trees, flowers, little plants, birds— is a constant presence in my verse, visible from the beginning, illustrated particularly well in *Range of Light*, which is among the best of my books, I think, as well as the most homogeneous. The topics include sweeping landscapes and small desert features such as verbena and cactus wrens. The unified vision it suggests embraces relationships between human beings and nature as I experience them but also what I imagine them to be among the pre-Columbian Anasazis and evinced by today's Hopi, Navajo, and Pueblo Indian tribes. The seashore and ocean are favorite settings for reflections on nature as experienced by human consciousness.

The theme of romantic love likewise occupies a considerable place in my poetry: love discovered and lived; love lost, then found again. Additional material is furnished by family members, as I have known them or imagined them (for instance, my grandmother when, as a young woman, she arrived in Saguache). Christian belief is introduced, frequently, most obviously in poems on medieval illuminations illustrating saints' lives. Painting and architecture, especially ecclesiastical, sculpture, music, and dance furnish material for many poems, which offer an example of intergeneric expression. (In *An Aesthetic Education and Other Stories*, the narratrix and certain other characters are either painters or art historians. In my critical writings on French literature, one finds considerations on the ideograms of Apollinaire and the art criticism of Beauvoir, Sartre, and others.)

A grim theme in my poetry, recurrent, is war. Almost every collection contains at least one poem referring to armed conflict. This historically masculine enterprise has affected humanity from early times; Herodotus believed that civilization was closely bound to war-making. It affects millions. I believe that collective violence is part of human character—of the Fall, if you wish—and will not be remedied by any means. With Uncle Jack's death and Elizabeth's experience in Europe, it touched my family. Certain war poems are among my best, I hold, especially the series in *Arm in Arm* that includes "Normandy, 7 August 1944" and "Phoebe, 1944."

Antithetical to the phenomenon of war is that of order. The cosmos, in its general regularity, appears to undergird our ideas of order, and bodies of religion and philosophy with which I am familiar acknowledge the cosmic example, even when chaos also must be taken into consideration. Writing *is* order, poetry especially, which has as its very being (even free verse) arrangement of givens in such a way that sense is proposed. Words scattered on the page, as though blown out by a cannon, would seem to disprove that claim; but readers do try to find some sort of meaning dispersed in them, and critics take on counterexamples as challenges. That's not my sort of poetry anyhow.[4]

As various poems in *Range of Light* suggest, things in themselves, the *thereness* of things (Heidegger's *Dasein*), "the very essence of things," as Constantin Brancusi said, are among my poetic obsessions. Inanimate natural objects, such as fruit, vegetables, and stones are often treated in connection to their *thingness*. They *exist*. Painting, photography, and poems can reveal that existence as it goes beyond utility. My poems on foodstuffs, mostly fruit, vegetables, fungi, and seafood, number more than forty. "Strawberries" was the first. They have to do much less with preparation and consumption than

---

[4] See in my study *Louisiana Poets: A Literary Guide* (of which Olivia McNeely Pass was co-author) the entries on André Codrescu and William Lavender.

with the raw existence of the food object, in isolation. But there are cultural dimensions also and, even more important, the necessary connection to bodies; implied always is the relationship among nourishment, the body, and what goes beyond the body—mind and consciousness. There are also restaurant poems, often stressing conviviality and friendship but featuring menu offerings also.

In addition to these concerns, my verse treats people, sketched or seen fleetingly or portrayed in detail. Certain collections resemble a gallery; sometimes these memoirs do too.

Catharine and Patric Savage, Winter 2008
Photograph by Olivia McNeely Pass.

Chapter Twelve

Islands of Our Years

O f the patterns and metaphors by which we perceive, measure, and relate our lives, one of the oldest and most insistent is that of the journey. Expressions such as "travel life's road" and "along our way" are stock elements of graduation ceremonies, sermons, and greeting cards; such words are spoken at weddings and murmured at funerals.

The literary-minded recall the wanderings of Odysseus and those of Aeneas; knights errant and the *matière de Bretagne*; and Shakespeare's passage from *Julius Caesar*, quoted in chapter four. They know that the picaresque novel arose out of such romances and adventure stories, and that numerous outstanding English novels are quasi-epics (*The Adventures of Tom Jones*, for instance), in the plots of which journeys and digressions from the journeys play a significant role. One of these masterpieces features a real voyage over perilous seas by an "everyman," as J. Paul Hunter called Robinson Crusoe, "a wanderer on a sea he does not understand," who is marooned for twenty-eight years——a story based perhaps on the real case of Alexander Selkirk and his island to the west of Chile.

If life can be felt, according to the pattern set by Odysseus in the "mid-earth sea," as travel through space and time, especially as a sea voyage (with the related metaphors of ports, storms, rocks, eddies, wreckage), then it is also strung with islands—those clusters of years, activities, connections that rise above the horizon and constitute stopping places, places of relief, of discovery sometimes, perhaps of danger. Literature is full of such islands. Shakespeare needed an isle (inspired by Bermuda, some believe) as the setting for *The Tempest*. Think too of *Treasure Island*, which has haunted boys' imaginations since 1883; think of *The Count of Monte Cristo* and the two islands that play a role in the adventure of Dantès. In American writing, there is scarcely any place more fundamental than the island in the Mississippi on which Huck Finn and Jim find themselves.

More broadly, the cities of civilization are islands, so to speak, some of them literally—"the isles of Greece, the isles of Greece" (Byron) and Sicily. I think also of the oases of the ancient Near East—gardens of art, science, and language surrounded by sand and desolation. Perhaps, on the other side of the world, the South Pacific islands should be mentioned, from which men in canoes or outriggers set sail or drifted eastward to the other hemisphere, where eventually they established pre-Columbian civilizations. The earth itself is a kind of isle in the universe, surrounded by waves of time and space, "islanded in its stream of stars," as Henry Beston wrote. Astronauts have remarked on its singular blue beauty. Like Saint-Exupéry's Little Prince, we are travelers, fallen from the skies, finding a home on our cosmic isle.

Or are we ourselves unmoored islands, floating masses of stuff like sargasso, half-directed by oar or rudder, half-driven by the winds of fate and the dark, unseen currents below? "No man is an island," preached John Donne; but Matthew Arnold, for whom the "sea of faith" had ebbed, wrote:

Yes! In the sea of life enisled,

With echoing straits between us thrown,

Dotting the shoreless watery wild,

We mortal millions live *alone*.[1]

The years since I moved to the Garden District and, not long thereafter, retired from Tulane constitute what the poet St-John Perse called "grand age" (although he was only sixty when he wrote of it). He was literally a man of islands, having been born on his family's own Caribbean island, spending his adolescence on nearby Guadeloupe, writing of isles over and over, calling his first published poetic series "Images à Crusoé." I see this time since 1992 as an archipelago, consisting of three periods. "The Garden District" traces the first. The second was defined by my email reconnection with Patric Savage in July 2007 and our remarriage a year later. He was my greatest island in the flow of years, loved early, loved again, loved still. That mankind is metaphysically alone, perhaps absolutely so, I concede as possible; but he and I were together on our island then. The third period, dating from his death in 2017, is another island, on which I am left to live without him.

The "human miracle" of that reconnection has been recounted elsewhere. The account, which Pat urged me to publish, cost us one friendship from my circle and two or three from Pat's. A reviewer praised the poems it accompanied but took us to task, harshly, for our conduct. His judgment strikes me as short-sighted. Should a Christian not practice forgiving and endeavor to see the hand of Providence in the mending of a broken circle? A devout Roman Catholic friend gave a theological reading to the story: we had been truly wed to each other from the beginning, and our remarriage simply resealed what we had broken. (What her theology would do with the daughter born of another husband I do not know.)[2]

Our years of happiness, though too few, were comfortable, serene, meaningful; we were secure in each other's love. But I must write about Pat's health. His lungs were not good; one had collapsed in 1958. Nor his heart. In California, he had a bilateral

---

[1]   "To Marguerite."
[2]   See the Postface to *Breakwater.*

infarction. A cardiologist named Shirey prescribed the drug heparin. Pat's condition worsened so that he was told to inform his friends and relatives and say goodbye. When his old Houston tennis partner Earl Beard, a prominent specialist, later co-chairman of the department at St. Luke's Hospital, learned of Pat's condition and the heparin, he demanded that the drug regimen be changed to Coumadin. It saved his life. But why would the California man agree? It turned out, providentially, that Earl had saved the lives of both Dr. Shirey's parents.

Once better, Pat secured a position with Shell Development in Houston, For the rest of his life, his drug regimen would include Coumadin but also other potent chemicals that did much collateral damage, doubtless. I am not qualified to question them. (Finally, Pat did so, demanding a lower dose of the worst.) At age sixty, he chose to retire, in order to read—and he did so, enormously, judiciously. He continued to cultivate his friendships and play tennis.[3]

In 2004, though, he collapsed on a tennis court. Emergency medical technicians thought his lungs were failing. Instead, an embolism ("the size of my thumb," he would say) was discovered in his heart. He was saved, barely in time. He also survived bladder cancer. His first fall following our marriage occurred late in 2009, leaving him flat on his back in the bedroom. He used a cane thenceforth. He was a good sport about it, as he was in everything. He ordered and organized his medications regularly, kept his doctors' appointments, and did not complain. Rather late, he had cataract surgery and therefore could drive at night.

Pat was very good to me, enduring with a smile my eccentricities and manias. "Funny animule," he would say to me, tenderly. Once he announced, "I love growing old with you." Most hours were spent in his condominium apartment, large enough, fortunately, to accommodate his piano and nearly thirty bookcases, plus adequate chairs for a party and a great marble dining table. Our peaceable domestic routine, good for each of us, included "dressing-gown"

---

[3]   See "Four Modes of Book Collecting" in *Music from the Lake and Other Essays* and "Pat Curating His Library" in *Arm in Arm*.

mornings and modest daytime meals at his kitchen table. We both liked classical music and listened often to recordings; he favored Spanish and baroque composers, but a few moderns also. He also fiddled with his own compositions, for piano, though one he turned into an oboe piece and had it recorded. He copied certain pieces for me or changed the key so that I could play or, in one instance, sing them better.

Another pleasure was looking at art books. Several shelves in his library held his collection, most in large format. He was interested in Leonardo and Cellini, Delacroix and Rodin, the Impressionists and Post-Impressionists. Gwen John was among those artists in whom he took particular interest. One of his volumes, *The Hours of Catherine de Cleves*, furnished the magnificent illuminations that inspired two series of short poems.[4]

After lunch, Pat normally had a nap, not on the bed but stretched out in his green leather chair with a hassock. He liked to pull a blanket over himself. (My siestas are on top of the bed—never under covers— but on occasion I likewise use one, since I rarely put on any heat.) I had passed on to him a red and blue extra-long blanket, handed down from Patricia Teed, whose son, Arthur, had used it in boarding school and college. It was functional—it still is available—but, made of acrylic, it is not very warm. I ordered for him from Pendleton an all-wool blanket. The day it arrived, I spread it on him at nap time. He said, 'I'm warmer already." Now I have it on my bed often.

Changing our setting, we spent the late afternoons and dinner hours in my condo, in the same building. I had settled there upon moving from New Orleans and, after our marriage, kept it as a work space, with its bookshelves, old family furniture, and Margo's baby grand. I often went up around 4:30 to practice. The kitchen was user-friendly to me, its pots and pans familiar, two or three my mother's. Returning after dinner to Pat's place, we arranged a program for the evening, usually a film from his vast collection. It included many called "classics." The one he admired above all others was Fellini's *La Strada*.

---

[4]   See *A Memory of Manaus* and *Arm in Arm*.

We had very good season seats for the Houston Ballet and Grand Opera. Earl Beard and his wife, Lovie, often invited us to the Racquet Club. We were entertained by friends and entertained them in turn. I recall how Pat would help me clean before guests came: I would vacuum the main rooms; he would straighten books and magazines and, using an old tennis sock (convenient), dust the furniture.

Since his choir boy days in St. Louis, Pat, whose tenor voice was very good, had enjoyed singing. He collected sheet music, subscribed to *Sheet Music Magazine*, looked up folk song archives to get words, and memorized many, along with opera arias and art songs. His large repertory included Irish songs in particular. I'll mention "Why Paddy's Not at Work Today" and a sad ballad about sailing to Botany Bay. Before our reconciliation, he had started singing for friends at parties; he had many fans. He sang for me at our wedding in 2008 and at home. He would break out in song sometimes as though he could keep in the tune no longer. At the house of his close friends Vijay and Florence Arya, he always did his version of "Granada," of which they and I were particular fans. He knew songs that I had taught him in the 1950s from Scout camp in Colorado: "Here Am I" and "Skyball Paint."

Often we drove to Rice, where I looked up a few things in the library and checked out books, Pat waiting patiently. Grateful for his virtually free education, he had been devoted to his alma mater. He had made generous contributions. They ceased when the university ceased, in his view, to deserve them. One chunk of money had earned him the status of "Rice Associate." Associates were entitled to a formal dinner from time to time and a library card, with one for the spouse. I daresay few took advantage of it. But that's how we had borrowing privileges; my own credentials did not suffice.

My little condo apartment in downtown Colorado Springs be-came our summer place; it was our island in the sky. I liked being in my mother's city, slightly on the east side but with the old north and west sides and Manitou Springs easily accessible. I could walk across downtown and to Colorado College. Many poems were in-spired by that setting, others composed there. We organized a few little gatherings, had house guests from out of state, and spent time with my maternal cousins. Each summer we attended a piano competition, with performers from abroad as well as the States. That is where we made the acquaintance of Mary McKinley and her friend the late Kathleen Finney, who had a fine mezzo-soprano voice, gave recitals from time to time, and sang informally with Pat.

Colorado Springs was a fine jumping-off place for road journeys, taking us sometimes to historic sites and affording splendid desert, montane, and alpine panoramas. We sought out the less-traveled roads and destinations such as the Great Dunes and the north rim of the Grand Canyon; but we went also to Mesa Verde. We were fond of old hotels built of timbers or stone. Access was not always easy; for Pat, full flights of stairs were ruled out. We enjoyed historic mountain establishments in Fairplay, Leadville, and Fort Collins.

We traveled elsewhere also. On a trip east we stayed at a rock-faced establishment in Granville, Ohio, where Pat managed to climb the stairs to our room. We flew to New York to see Kate and her family, drove to the southern Atlantic states, and visited New Orleans, where we held parties at the Columns Hotel. And we went abroad, starting with a visit in November 2008 to Ireland, Scotland, and England. Not all plans were fulfilled. In spring 2010, we planned a personalized luxury trip through Spain, including Granada. Pat was an admirer of Washington Irving and collected editions of his works. The Alhambra was to be the highlight of the journey. At Eastertime, though, he was hospitalized for irregular heartbeat. The cardiologist (Earl's successor), learning of our plans to visit Spain, told Pat to cancel them. The fellow may have thought Pat should not fly (there or anywhere) because of the changes in air pressure, or perhaps he had no confidence in Spanish doctors. Ironic, if that's so; he himself was a foreigner.

We took our first cruise together at the end of 2011. Pat had some experience of the sea on navy ships in his NROTC days and cruises around Norway. Yet he did not foresee how much he would enjoy our thirty days. We sailed from Ft. Lauderdale through the Antillles, crossed through the Panama Canal, visited Colombia and Ecuador briefly, then Peru for three nights, and, turning north, sailed up the west coast of Central America and Mexico to San Diego.

As illness, or the doctor, had foreclosed the journey to Spain, it gave particular shape to that first cruise. Since flying was forbidden, we took trains. The route was circuitous. We first got on an Amtrak bus to Longview, Texas, to get the Texas Eagle, bound from San Antonio for Chicago. I recall the packed waiting room in Longview, where I had to intervene to get an able-bodied person to give Pat a seat. (Not the only occasion.)

Reaching Chicago in late morning, we had nearly a day's layover. My friend Dragana Pajic (with whom we later enjoyed, to the degree possible, a deplorable hotel you will read about) met us and took us to a comfortable restaurant near the station, then accompanied us back, leaving us in the first-class lounge to await the train to Washington, likewise an overnighter. I recall waking to see buildings, indeed a whole town, of old red brick; we were on the East Coast. After another wait in D.C., we boarded a third overnight train for Florida. Once there, we had to spend a night at a hotel before sailing the next day.

On the return journey, we disembarked in San Diego, where we boarded a train to Los Angeles. Some hours later, we got on the Sunset Limited. That sleek train, which I had ridden for twelve hours each way as a Rice undergraduate, makes few stops; one is Alpine. Pat was moved, more than I, by the thought of seeing the surrounding landscape and the town, which he had not revisited for decades. He wanted to get off, briefly. Indeed; the pause lasts no more than two or three minutes. He managed the steps, looked around at the station and businesses along Highway 90, walked a few paces, and got back on, almost nimbly. His memory must have been full of images from his first visit there (at New Year's 1955, before our marriage), meeting my parents, establishing his connection with the Chihuahua Desert. His emotion was a tribute.

In summer 2012, driving from Ohio to Colorado, Pat and I stopped in St. Louis to visit his parents' graves in a national military cemetery. It was a moving moment. In 2014, we visited those of my parents. The following account will be long; the distances out west are long and daylight likewise in most of the Trans-Pecos area—on Central Time despite being very far west. The previous day we had driven through New Mexico south to El Paso, where we stayed with Pat's friends Larry and Norma Price. They dine late. The delicious Mexican food did not sit well with Pat. Leaving El Paso, later than we'd wished, we headed for Van Horn (about 120 miles). As we hummed along Interstate 10 (speed limit 80 mph), suddenly Pat felt an urgent need. I managed to pull over and stop; we climbed a short rise. No trees at all; just scrub mesquite, creosote bush, and cacti. I handed him a roll of toilet paper, and he found a rock behind which he concealed himself a bit. At a service station in Van Horn we pulled into a convenience store so that he could wash up. He threw in a trash can his fine peppermint-candy-striped shorts.

Van Horn is the western terminus of US 90. It comes in from the southeast. Most drivers continue east on I-10, but Pat said, "Let's leave the interstate and drive to Alpine instead, so that we can visit the cemetery." The distance was ninety-nine miles. In that nearly deserted territory, some rather level, the rest mountainous, driving is easy: few towns, little traffic. Still, time is required for the curves and inclines. At two o'clock, when we reached Marfa, I was famished. The Paisano Hotel, famous during the filming of *Giant*, beckoned. Alas, the dining room had closed. Where else can one find a decent lunch? It took quite a while (though it's a very small town) to locate anything but a fast-food place and, once we found one, still longer to get the food. Twenty-six more miles led us to Alpine.

We did not make a detour to see my parents' house; I drove straight to the cemetery. The September heat was fierce. No custodian was around, and the posted outline of paths and plots was unintelligible. Driving along, I recognized, by some grace, the pink granite markers on my parents' graves. I urged Pat to stay in the car, with the air-conditioning on; he heeded me. I spent a few minutes brushing sand from the stones and meditating. Prudently, once back in the car, I called a chain motel in Del Rio to book a room. We reached the town, a distance of 199 miles, in darkness, around 8:30 We were whipped. But, again, Pat had initiated the tribute. I shall never forget it.[5]

It was Pat who wanted to sign up for a sixty-two-day circumnavigation of South America, from early January to March 2013, starting in Florida, through the Caribbean islands and the Panama Canal, down the west coast of South America and into Antarctic waters, then north along the east coast, into the Antilles again, and back to Florida. By then he had decided to defy the order against flying.

What a marvelous adventure that was! Among its benefits was getting acquainted with Loren and Janie Slye, of Steveston (greater Vancouver), whose company was delightful. They escorted me around on land sometimes when Pat chose not to go. A photograph shows two smiling couples on deck, with hands together or arms around shoulders. The ship, the smallest Holland America vessel, under the command of a British captain, was much to our liking. What did we do all that time? We worked the daily crossword together each morning, walked around and chatted with other travelers, read, looked out from our veranda on the water and every port, and enjoyed our meals. I wrote on a mini-laptop.

A dust-up in the Caribbean produced rough waters, the worst we encountered, and we missed going ashore on Robinson Crusoe Island—the seas were not friendly enough. Otherwise we were favored by the weather. In Punta Arenas, Chile, a base for Saint-Exupéry at one time, the famous strong winds, so dangerous for little planes, did appear on cue, but only 50 mph that day. I got ashore (Pat declined to test his balance on the swaying gangway), and, holding onto ropes, walked around the square. The Straits of Magellan were calm. As for the Antarctic waters and their icebergs, we were not disappointed; the powerful blue of deep ice was gorgeous. Port calls at the Falkland Islands and Buenos Aires—three nights, at two piers, thus two visions—were among my favorites.[45]

More cruises followed. We did a forty-two day Far East voyage in 2015, from Southampton to Singapore. In the second port of call,

---

5   Poems that reflect these stops are "At Jefferson Barracks Cemetery" in *On the Old Plaza* and "An Epitaph for My Parents' Graves" in *A Memory of Manaus*.

Málaga, Pat took a terrific tumble down a high escalator in the cruise terminal. He was rescued and saved from being immobilized in a Spanish hospital when the ship's doctor came with a wheelchair and got him back on shipboard. Black and blue all along his right side and in considerable discomfort, he was treated daily by the medical staff for three weeks or so. He gave those nurses a *raison d'être*. Soldiering on, he joined me in paid excursions at every port save one.

In February 2014, during a New York school winter vacation, Kate and her family accompanied us for a week in the Western Caribbean, out of Galveston. In August 2016 we invited them to join us a two-week adventure through the Inland Passage to Alaska and back. Two nights before we were to fly from Denver to Seattle, Pat fell in the bathroom. Again, he was black and blue and aching. Should we give up? I urged him to, insisting that the Deimlings could go anyhow. Oh, no!

The Denver airport, which we reached by a shuttle van, is not friendly. Ask anyone who's been there. From the shuttle stop we had to walk, without assistance (since the wheelchairs are kept inside, at the counters) and with all our luggage, to the Delta counter, the farthest from the entrance. Two women employees were there. Seeing us, they started exclaiming and soon fell all over Pat, admiring his sports coat, taking his luggage, giving encouragement; one even kissed him and said she'd like to take him home! Of course a chair was fetched immediately.

Off to Security and the gate, then inside the plane. Only when we were seated, with doors closed, did Pat realize that the wheelchair attendant had not retrieved his cane from the X-ray belt. Too late. In a Seattle drugstore I bought an ordinary Medicare cane for him, but, even adjusted for length, it was too short; he spent two weeks bent over it, in visible discomfort. Yet he went to meals regularly, enjoying the company of Kate's family and the view from our dinner table at the stern, by the wake. (The cane was retrieved and ultimately shipped to us by FedEx.)

Our final travel adventure took place in the autumn of 2016, Pat's last. The destination was the Clocktower Hotel and Resort in

Rockford, Illinois, a medium-sized industrial city. What, a "resort"? No native palm trees, no seashore, no surfboards or ski-jets. But for some who cannot afford to go find pleasure in Florida or the Antilles, it offered a simulacrum: water slide and swimming pool, bars and eateries. It had one advantage for us: a shuttle bus from O'Hare airport to Rockford stops there. Correction: it doesn't stop there anymore.

The establishment was spread out, mostly on the ground floor. It had a pub at one end, conference rooms at the opposite end, and, in between, shops (some closed), a beauty salon, and an Asian restaurant. Upon arriving, Pat felt stiff. Even with his cane, he found walking from the bus drop-off near the pub to the lobby and registration desk quite tiring. We were assigned to a room requiring walking up a few steps—no elevator in that section. We noticed two policemen. Good; we would be safe! A fireman appeared also. Hmm. At 5:00 we went to an informal reception, met Dragana again, ate with her in the pub, and called it a day.

The following morning, policemen and firemen were again on the premises. Pat and I attended the first conference sessions, had lunch in the pub, and returned to the conference room for the afternoon. As someone was speaking, Pat nudged me, then got up and left. He did not return promptly. More time passed, then more; a new speaker took over. I no longer know how long I waited for him. Might he have fallen? Perfectly plausible. But I did nothing. That's just as well. Finally, he reappeared and took his seat.

What had happened? I shall sketch it as delicately as possible. He had not made it to the men's room in time. His trousers served, partially; the carpet took the rest, as two workers arriving just then to vacuum the lobby discovered. He had hobbled upstairs, undressed, and, without the aid of grab-bars, climbed into the tub-shower. Risky; but he was desperate. He had washed himself, dealt with his shorts and trousers, gotten out, and dressed in dry clothes and returned. Poor darling! I think he was not quite the same that evening. Was there crude symbolism in that incident, a comment on the establishment?

The next morning, when the conference ended, we learned that the previous weekend, at a crowded, rather rowdy gathering of pleasure-seekers, someone committed a murder, in public. To guard against a recurrence seemed irrational. The revelers had departed, the body had been removed, and I presume that the perpetrator had fled or been apprehended. A copycat murder struck me as a preposterous supposition. Still, police and a firefighter were present. Who decided that we, attending the conference, would not be told what had occurred? Who let it out the morning of our departure? The buildings were razed some months later. We could not be sorry.

Pat fell six or seven times that year (2016), then again at the beginning of the new year. We took two little Texas trips that winter, however, one to Austin to visit Patricia Teed, the other to Waco, for the St. Patrick's Day party given by the Department of Political Science, under the headship of David Clinton. That party was a tradition; we'd been invited before. Pat always wore his fine bespoke green wool jacket, and he always sang. If no rain threatened the merrymaking, everything took place outside. I picture him now in the patio, surrounded by circles of listeners.

Why did we do everything I've traced in this chapter? Why not go home and wait quietly to die? All that money could be given to the poor. What, though, would the poor do with it? Perhaps pay bills for essentials. Just as likely, if they are subsidized, they would buy larger television screens and, maybe, travel. We are given time and bodies to be used—enjoyed, if possible, certainly not put on a shelf. We may be merely winds, variously gusts and zephyrs; but, even, we are here to move and be moved.

I have quoted Pat as saying, *pace* Aristotle, "I'm a happy man." (Believing that the Moirae, or Fates, were the most powerful of gods, the great philosopher recommended that one not pronounce on a life until it is closed.) Pat was happy; he knew it and appreciated it. The happiness would not be destroyed, though it would, inevitably, end.

At the end of March, he had an infection, then a fall, followed by two further falls in quick succession, emergency room visits, and a second, dangerous infection, undiagnosed until he was admitted to a skilled nursing facility. Though it yielded to antibiotics, his organs were failing. When he lost interest in reading, I could measure his decline. You do not want to read more about the last weeks and months in that place, which he left for a hospital, hospice, and mortuary.

During my final visit to the hospice, he spoke very little. I tried to comfort him, stroking this arm. It occurred to me to sing something. "Juanita" was the choice. The next morning, he died. Half-unconscious with grief, I went nevertheless to have a PT test connected to the treatment of the non-Hodgkins lymphoma that had gotten me, my portion of that year of physical suffering. (My mind would never give way, as I have noted, so my body did.) Arranging for burial was difficult. Pat wished to be interred in his army uniform in a national cemetery. Federal officials take their time. Soon Hurricane Harvey was chewing up parts of the Mexican coast. It arrived in Texas downgraded to a tropical storm but with a tremendous amount of water to be dumped onto us. No one was buried in Houston then.

Finally, on the 6th of September, a grave could be dug, and servicemen were released from storm-related duty for the ceremony, held at a small pavilion outdoors. Two sets of friends could not leave their flooded neighborhoods to attend. But the sky was of jewel blue. Everything proceeded with solemnity—presentation of arms, folding of the flag draped over the coffin, reading of the poem by Henry Lee quoted in chapter four, a beautiful unaccompanied singing by Megan Conway of "The Little Minstrel Boy," and taps.

For these years after Pat's death, I must be grateful, although it is bittersweet to be a survivor, I thank God and my good parents, as well as doctors who cured me and researchers behind them. One supposes that those no longer with us want us to live on and live well—to remember them, carry on some legacy, perhaps, or simply be happy. Churches and Jewish congregations speak of the importance of valuing our own lives even as we mourn the loss of others. Pat had a huge spirit. I try to maintain a bit of it in myself.

The remainder of this memoir is an afterlife. Pat and I had planned to go to Colorado in summer 2017 and spend a week at a dude ranch with the Deimlings. Instead, they came to Houston. In 2018, I drove to Colorado Springs in the big red Chevy that we bought in '16, easy for Pat to get into and roomy enough for everyone. We did have an outstanding week at the ranch. My drive back to Texas was taxing, however. What had happened to my eyes, my endurance? I gave up highway driving, then stopped entirely, and, with regret, sold the Colorado property. I think of the southern arteries I know so well, US 90, I-10, and the countless roads I've taken elsewhere in the Lower 48. But I'm riding on the age of ninety.[6]

I have not renounced friendships with men. Readers of *Aerosols* will have noticed a nascent love affair with a very presentable, qualified man some years younger than I. (Any man my age would be far too old.) It remained platonic and, despite evidence of compatibility, particularly love of books and ideas, and strong suggestions of interest, it went nowhere. No matter. It had nothing to do with my love for Pat and devotion to his memory. But he is dead and I am not. No sequel will come, however. That was my last shot. It was a good one; it circled the basket with energy, only to fall out. The buzzer sounded; game over.

I am left, some seven years after Pat was buried, to live much as we lived before—except, alas, without him. It seems a very long time since I saw him, heard his voice, and felt his vitality. Now older than he was at the end of his life, I am fortunate to be in good health and feel young. I use makeup and do not wear old women's clothes nor orthopedic shoes. I do not need any of these fashionable tattoos on my hands; the blue veins make nice patterns.

For a professional society, I do, remotely, a small amount of volunteer work connected to literature. The Deimlings and I see each other as often as our schedules and the distances between us allow. My regard for all four is high, and I am pleased that, starting in autumn 2024, both Clara and Julian will be at their mother's alma mater, the University of Chicago. Margo's piano gets frequent

---

[6] See "Road Nostalgia" in *Aerosols.*

attention. The hymnal falls open easily to a page, uniformly yellowed, left exposed in the past to cigar smoke. I play from a student's book dating from days with Aunt Mary—Bach, Beethoven, Boccherini, Handel, Massenet. To that old repertory I've added a William Byrd "Ave verum corpus" and pieces Pat recommended or taught me. He played better than I, but I was more skilled at sightreading. He'd had no training as a boy but at age fifty started lessons.

In September 2021, as Jack and Jeannie Miller and I were approaching New Orleans in their car from Paradis, Des Allemands, and Boutté, they remarked, "You seem so happy here!" Now, I am a happy person generally, as happy as possible after losing the man I call my "great companion." Nevertheless, some new spirit had manifested itself in me. We crossed the Huey P. Long Bridge and took the Jefferson Highway into New Orleans, then drove a bit around the Carrollton and University neighborhoods. Jack said, "Why don't you buy yourself a place here?" The question answered itself. After their departure for points north, I left the hotel and went to stay with Michèle and Everett Beelman. They have realtor's licenses. "Michèle, could you find me something?"[7]

She did; so I am often in a little condo at the back of The Carol, on the streetcar line, at the corner of St. Charles Avenue and Jackson. Built in 1966, it advertises the decade—like those 60s buildings in England that many observers would like to raze but cannot, since they are protected. But from my desk I can see a fine sycamore and a palm; and if I lean a bit, a portion of the Eiffel Tower shipped to New Orleans and rebuilt as a party venue. Furthermore, my place has attractive accent colors, a Dhurrie rug, and pleasing art on the walls. Joseph Warner calls it "zen." Hearing me speak of it, an acquaintance elsewhere who had read *The Confederacy of Dunces* inquired, "Would Ignatius Reilly approve of your place?" "Oh, yes," I replied, "it overlooks the trash bins." It's plain that my connection to New Orleans is good, almost visceral. Think of it: some of Samuel Beckett's stage characters are *in* rubbish bins, and they discourse on life pretty well!

---

[7] See "Blue Tarpaulins" and "Avery Island" in *Aerosols and Other Poems*.

In 2023, I accepted an invitation to travel with a Houston acquaintance, Richard Meisch, to Gråsten, Denmark, to visit our mutual friend, Lotte Optekamp, for whose hospitality I am grateful. Our plans included four nights in Paris for all three. Lotte proposed going by train, through Hamburg. Ah, that thought pleased me greatly! It was for poetic reasons, as I recalled with admiration—no, with a shiver of awe, a sense of drama—the adventure in the port of Hamburg, on a foggy night, roughly a hundred years previously, of St. John Perse. For years I had wanted to see that port, poetically, in the fog, and in the year 1923! Quite impossible. So, in bright sunshine, we took a tourist boat to see the miles-long port installations, with their gigantic cranes, along both banks of the Elbe. It all contrasted strikingly with what Leger described as he made his way to the docks, with difficulty, in the rain and fog, coming upon an ancient ship he visited by gangplank and an ancient mariner playing on an old foot-pedal organ. Pointing to the deck, the old sailor showed him, under a pile of blankets, what he called "the child"—his dying companion, a monkey, trembling, with matted fur. In my poem on the incident, I evoked

> flesh, its terror immemorial, and lifelines cast
>
> in darkness over the abyss—the grace of Handel's
>
> music played by an old navigator, knotty
>
> fingers pointing to a death bed, and the fiercer cry
>
> of poetry, bright aerolites roping across the skies...[8]

In 1946, Simone de Beauvoir published a novel called *Tous les hommes sont mortels*, a modern fable concerning the need for death. A recent author, Andrew Stark, has taken up the theme in *The Consolations of Mortality*. Such works, of little value to the young and strong, may mean little even to a "senior" who has reasonably good health and interesting acquaintances. But they must be better

---

[8] See "Leger in Hamburg" in *Under the Pergola.*

than what the philosopher Grafton Tanner examines in *Foreverism*, which surveys attempts to use so-called artificial intelligence to reproduce the deceased, by algorithms, for survivors' pleasure. We would enter into conversations with holographic versions of the dead, hear their laughter, reminisce with them. No, thank you.

Can I keep at it? For a while, for a while. *Chaque chose en son temps.* Old players need to emulate Archie Manning, the first, and longtime, quarterback of the New Orleans Saints, and the unrivaled George Blanda, who played for twenty-six seasons: when the knees go bad from use, when the body recoils from being sacked once again, use your intelligence and experience. I think of my grandparents. I sound the years, as the old sea captains of yore sounded the seas. The logbook will close in due course. Like Gide's Theseus, "J'ai fait mon oeuvre" (I have done my work).

Readers, do you like these reminiscences and lives reflected therein? Do you like your stories? Recount them, to yourself to start with, to put them into order, and then to others.

Je, soussigné...("I, the undersigned.") The formula, ungrammatical, is inherited from ages ago. It attests to identity and knowledge thereof. That is the best one can do.

Catharine

Houston and New Orleans

23 November 2023—4 May 2024

Scholarly Works by Catharine Savage Brosman

French Literature

André Gide: l'évolution de sa pensée religieuse (Paris: Nizet, 1962);

Malraux, Sartre, and Aragon as Political Novelists (Gainesville: University of Florida Press, 1964);

Roger Martin du Gard (New York: Twayne Publishers, 1968);

Jean-Paul Sartre (Boston: Twayne Publishers, 1983; rpt., 1984);

Jules Roy (Philadelphia: Celfan Edition Monographs, 1988);

French Novelists, 1900-1930 (Dictionary of Literary Biography, 65), ed. with a foreword (Detroit: Gale, l988);

French Novelists, 1930-1960 (Dictionary of Literary Biography, 72), ed. with a foreword (Detroit: Gale, 1988);

French Novelists since 1960 (Dictionary of Literary Biography, 83), ed. with a foreword (Detroit: Gale, 1989);

Art as Testimony: The Work of Jules Roy (Gainesville: University of Florida Press, 1989);

An Annotated Bibliography of Criticism on André Gide, 1973-1988 (New York: Garland Publishing, 1990);

Simone de Beauvoir Revisited (Boston: Twayne, 1991);

Nineteenth-Century French Fiction Writers, 1800-1860: Romantics and Realists (Dictionary of Literary Biography, 119), ed. with an introduction (Detroit: Gale, 1992);

Nineteenth-Century French Fiction Writers, 1860-1900: Naturalists and Beyond (Dictionary of Literary Biography, 123), ed. with an introduction (Detroit: Gale, 1992);

Twentieth-Century French Culture, 1900-1975, ed. with an introduction (Detroit: Gale, 1995);

Retour aux "Nourritures terrestres": Le Centenaire d'un bréviaire, ed. David H. Walker and Catharine Savage Brosman (Amsterdam: Rodopi, 1997);

Visions of War in France: Fiction, Art, Ideology (Baton Rouge: Louisiana State University Press, 1999; rpt., Boulder:Net Library2001);

Existential Fiction (Detroit: Gale, 2000);

Albert Camus (Detroit: Gale, 2000).

American Literature

Louisiana Creole Literature: A Historical Study (Jackson: University Press of Mississippi, 2013; rpt., 2024);

Southwestern Women Writers and the Vision of Goodness (Jefferson, NC: McFarland and Co., 2016);

Louisiana Poets: A Literary Guide (with Olivia McNeely Pass) (Jackson: University Press of Mississippi, 2019);

Mississippi Poets: A Literary Guide (Jackson: University Press of Mississippi, 2020).

AVAILABLE FROM GREEN ALTAR BOOKS

If you enjoyed this book, perhaps some of our other titles will pique your interest. The following titles are now available for your reading pleasure... Enjoy!

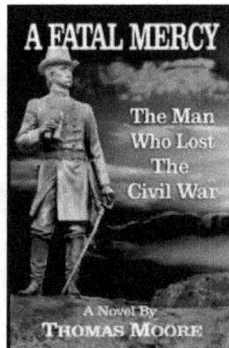

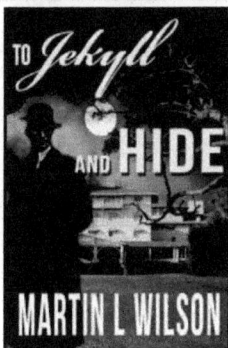

GA
GREEN ALTAR BOOKS
SHOTWELL PUBLISHING

Green Altar (Literary Imprint)

CATHARINE SAVAGE BROSMAN
*An Aesthetic Education
and Other Stories (2nd Ed)*

Chained Tree, Chained Owls: Poems

Aerosols and Other Poems

Partial Memoirs

RANDALL IVEY
*A New England Romance:
And Other Southern Stories*

The Gift of Gab

SUZANNE JOHNSON
Maxcy Gregg's Sporting Journals 1842-1858

JAMES E. KIBLER, JR.
Tiller : Claybank County Series, Vol. 4

The Gentler Gamester

*In the Deep Heart's Core: Poems of Tribute and
Remembrance (forthcoming)*

THOMAS MOORE
*A Fatal Mercy:
The Man Who Lost The Civil War*

PERRIN LOVETT
The Substitute, Tom Ironsides 1

KAREN STOKES
Belles

Carolina Twilight

Honor in the Dust

The Immortals

The Soldier's Ghost: A Tale of Charleston

WILLIAM THOMAS
*Runaway Haley:
An Imagined Family Saga*

*The Field of Justice: Moonshine
and Murder in North Georgia*

CLYDE N. WILSON
*Southern Poets and Poems, 1606-1860:
The Land They Loved, Volume 1*

*Confederate Poets and Poems, Vol 1
The Land They Loved, Volume II*

Gold-Bug
(Mystery & Suspense Imprint)

BRANDI PERRY
Splintered: A New Orleans Tale

MARTIN WILSON
To Jekyll and Hide

www.ingramcontent.com/pod-product-compliance
Lightning Source LLC
Chambersburg PA
CBHW060049100426
42742CB00014B/2749